Judy Garton-Sprenger and Philip Prowse
with Helena Gomm and Catrin Morris

1 TURNING POINTS

1 How are you feeling?

1 Reading

Read the interview and complete the sentences.

INTERVIEWER Hi, Sophie. Do you live in London?
SOPHIE No, I don't. I live in Liverpool.
INTERVIEWER Are you still at school?
SOPHIE Yes, I am.
INTERVIEWER What are your favourite subjects?
SOPHIE Biology and Spanish.
INTERVIEWER Spanish? Do you speak any other languages?
SOPHIE No, I don't.
INTERVIEWER What do you usually do at weekends?
SOPHIE I work in a shoe shop every Saturday and I often go to clubs with my friends on Saturday night. Or we listen to music and play video games.
INTERVIEWER What's your ambition?
SOPHIE I want to be a doctor and I'd like to travel around South America.

1 Sophie _lives_ in Liverpool.
   She _doesn't_ live in London.
2 She _____ English and Spanish. She _____ speak any other languages.
3 She _____ in a shoe shop every Saturday.
4 On Saturday night, Sophie and her friends often _____ out or _____ video games.
5 Sophie _____ to be a doctor.

2 Present continuous questions and short answers

Write questions and short answers using the present continuous.

1 Rob/read anything at the moment ✘
   Is Rob reading anything at the moment?
   No, he isn't.
2 he/feel excited ✔
3 he/wear jeans ✔
4 Rob's friends/wait for him ✘
5 Rob/look forward to the holidays ✔
6 he/look for a girlfriend ✘

3 Present simple and present continuous

Complete Sophie's email with the present simple or present continuous of these verbs.

be (x3)   eat   go   have   love   stay   want   work   write

From: Sophie
To: Jen
Subject: Barcelona!

Hi Jen,
We (1) _____ here at last! And Barcelona (2) _____ a brilliant place. We (3) _____ here for two days and then we (4) _____ to Madrid. Our hotel (5) _____ close to Parc Güell and it (6) _____ a great view. Our tour guide is called Pablo. He is really nice. He (7) _____ to be a doctor, but at the moment he (8) _____ as a guide to make some money. I (9) _____ this in a café near Las Ramblas and I (10) _____ an ice cream at the same time. I (11) _____ Barcelona!
Best wishes
Sophie

4 Present simple and present continuous

Complete the questions with the present simple or present continuous. Then answer the questions for yourself.

1 What _do_ you usually _do_ (do) on Saturday nights?
   I go to the cinema with my friends.
2 How often _____ you _____ (watch) TV each week?
3 Where _____ you _____ (sit) at the moment?
4 Who _____ you usually _____ (talk) to at school?
5 What _____ you _____ (look) forward to doing this weekend?

5 Present continuous for future arrangements

Rob is talking to his friend, Jake, on the phone. Complete the dialogue with these verbs.

come   have   help   meet   play   watch

JAKE Hi, Rob! My mate Dave (**1**) .... to see me tomorrow. Let's have coffee or a meal together.

ROB Great idea – but I'm quite busy. I (**2**) .... my father until ten o'clock and then I (**3**) .... Jim at the sports centre. We (**4**) .... tennis.

JAKE Cool. We can meet after that.

ROB I (**5**) .... lunch with Jim after the game. How about in the afternoon?

JAKE Sure. We (**6**) .... the football match on TV at three but after that is fine.

6 Adverbial phrases of frequency

Match the phrases in list A with the phrases in list B.

	A	B
1	every day	52 times a year
2	twice a week	twice a month
3	every two weeks	every 24 hours
4	every four months	12 times a year
5	every week	eight times a month
6	every month	three times a year

7 Vocabulary

Find seven words for things you wear in the word square.

T	R	A	I	N	E	R	S	L
Z	B	F	G	I	D	S	C	H
B	R	L	C	H	N	K	M	O
O	F	E	Y	S	D	I	O	O
O	I	E	S	H	I	R	T	D
T	T	C	U	W	E	T	O	I
S	J	E	A	N	S	L	P	E

8 Vocabulary

Match the words in list A with the words in list B and write eight compound nouns.

	A	B	
1	street	friend	*street crime*
2	sixth form	term	
3	science	trip	
4	girl	shop	
5	half	crime	
6	part	fiction	
7	shoe	college	
8	school	time	

9 Pronunciation

Do they rhyme (✔) or not (✘)?

1	care	hair	✔
2	crime	time	☐
3	fed	said	☐
4	half	laugh	☐
5	mate	wait	☐
6	work	talk	☐
7	term	worm	☐
8	worry	hurry	☐

Extension Write sentences in your notebook answering four of the questions in the *Teenage Life* questionnaire on page 10 of the Student's Book.

1 TURNING POINTS

2 Why didn't I enjoy it more?

From: Sara
To: Emily
Subject: Holiday problems

Dear Emily,
It's the third day of our holiday in Newquay, but I'm afraid things aren't going very well. I met some great people on the first day and I made friends at once. But Joni didn't like my new friends at all. She made new friends too and now spends all her time with them. To tell you the truth, I think her friends are really boring.
I don't know what's the matter with Joni. Yesterday evening I asked her to come to the cinema with us, but she went to a party instead. Her mother phoned her this morning – I heard Joni say 'see you soon, Mum'. Perhaps she's going home early – that doesn't bother me at all.
More later.
Love,
Sara

1 Reading

Read Sara's email. Then read the sentences and write T (true) or F (false). Correct the false sentences.

1 Sara and Emily are on holiday in Newquay. ☐

2 Sara and Joni both made new friends. ☐

3 Sara and Joni went to the cinema together yesterday. ☐

4 Sara saw Joni's mother at a party. ☐

5 Joni talked to her mother on the phone. ☐

2 Past simple of *be*

Complete with *was/were* or *wasn't/weren't*.

1 Joni and Sara _____ on holiday in London – they _____ on holiday in Newquay.

2 _____ Joni pleased to hear her mother's voice? Yes, she _____ .

3 Joni's parents _____ on holiday with her.

4 Joni and Sara _____ both excited before the start of the holiday.

5 It _____ a great place for a holiday but Joni _____ happy.

6 Sara and Joni _____ together at all – they _____ with their new friends all the time.

7 _____ Sara happy? No, she _____ .

3 Past simple questions, negative and short answers

Write questions and answers.

1 Joni/go on holiday in June/July
   Did Joni go on holiday in June?
   No, she didn't. She went on holiday in July.

2 Joni's mum/apologise for writing/phoning

3 Joni/want to stay in Newquay/go home

4 Joni/meet her friends in a disco/club

5 Joni/nearly cry when she heard her father's voice/ mother's voice

6 Joni/fall asleep at the party/on the beach

7 Joni/have a picnic with Sara/some friends

8 Joni/go for a swim in the pool/sea

UNIT 1

4 Past simple

Write questions about last weekend and answer them for yourself.

1 make a new friend
   Did you make a new friend?
   Yes, I did. He/She ... /No, I didn't.

2 phone someone

3 spend time with your friends

4 go for a swim

5 have a picnic

6 help your parents

5 Vocabulary

Complete the sentences with the adjectives for feelings.

> bored cheerful embarrassed excited
> lonely miserable pleased scared

1 Don't scream! It's just a spider. Are you really _____ of it?

2 There was no one interesting to talk to at the party, so I was _____.

3 Joni was very _____ about her first holiday without her parents.

4 Don't look so sad! Why can't you be more _____?

5 She was very _____ to hear her mother's voice – it made her very happy.

6 I felt so _____ when I couldn't remember his name.

7 When I moved to a new school I was very _____ for the first few weeks because I didn't know anyone.

8 What's the matter? You look so unhappy! Why are you feeling _____?

6 Vocabulary

Match the verbs with these words and phrases.

> a picnic all night angry asleep
> for a swim hello someone

1 fall
2 feel
3 go
4 have
5 last
6 miss
7 say

7 Vocabulary

Match the verbs in list A with the words and phrases in list B. Then write the phrases.

	A	B	
1	spend	round	1 *spend time*
2	have	time	2
3	make	depressed	3
4	mean	a good time	4
5	sound	new friends	5
6	turn	something to someone	6

8 Spelling

The same letter is missing in each line. Write the complete words.

1 plae   fantasti   exited
2 lonly   somone   frindship
3 everyting   togeter   pone
4 hrbour   plesed   miserble
5 embarrased mised   depresed
6 riht   enouh   niht

9 Pronunciation

Mark the stressed syllable.

■
asleep cheerful depressed embarrassed excited
fantastic friendship miserable surfing together
yesterday

> **Extension** Write five sentences in your notebook about what you did last weekend.

5

1 TURNING POINTS

3 She was surfing

1 Reading

Read the article and complete it with the past continuous of the verbs in brackets.

SHARK ATTACK

The shark attacked Bethany when she and her best friend Alana (1) _____ (surf) together. The two girls (2) _____ (hope) for a big wave. They certainly (3) _____ (not think) about a shark attack. Bethany (4) _____ (wait) on her board with her left hand in the water when the shark attacked. After the attack, she saw that she (5) _____ (lose) a lot of blood. Alana, her brother and her father helped Bethany to the beach. It took 15 minutes and all the time Bethany (6) _____ (say) to herself 'Get to the beach'. She (7) _____ (not try) to escape from the shark – she just wanted to get to the beach. Alana's father talked to her all the way to the beach. 'I (8) _____ (answer) all his questions', Bethany said afterwards, 'but I can't remember now what I said.'

2 Past simple and past continuous

What were they doing when the balloon landed? Write questions and answers using these phrases.

eat an ice cream   play football   ~~read a newspaper~~   skateboard   sunbathe

What was Anna doing when the balloon landed?
She was reading a newspaper.

What did they do when the balloon landed? Write sentences using these phrases.

fall off   not notice   phone a friend   say hello   ~~take a photo~~   wave

When the balloon landed, Anna took a photo.

UNIT 1

3 Past simple and past continuous

Write sentences about Tiffany and Jake as in the example. Use these phrases in the past simple or past continuous.

bring her some flowers   come to see him   ~~dance~~
fall asleep   paint a picture   phone him   read
sit in the park   start to rain   ~~take a photo~~
talk to her friends   watch football on TV

1 Tiffany was dancing when Jake took a photo.

2

3

4

5

6

4 Vocabulary

Complete the sentences with these words to make phrasal verbs with *get*.

away   back   on   out   over

1 Do you get .... well with your parents?
2 Shane was lucky to get .... from the crocodile.
3 We must get .... home in time for dinner.
4 Bethany got .... the accident very quickly.
5 Get .... of the pool, children, it's time for lunch.

5 Crossword

Complete the crossword and find this word ↓.

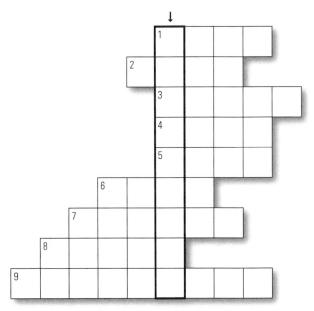

1 Move in water using arms and legs.
2 Use waves and a board to move in water.
3 The Thames is London's …
4 A shark is a kind of …
5 You travel on water in it.
6 You can swim in a swimming …
7 What happens when you dive or jump into 6.
8 You can see into water when it is …
9 It has lots of teeth and lives in water in hot countries.

6 Pronunciation

Circle the two rhyming words in each line.

1 (bright)   (white)   eight
2 here   clear   chair
3 hour   four   jaw
4 thought   shout   caught
5 water   daughter   later
6 turning   morning   warning
7 seem   scream   same
8 splash   wash   trash

> **Extension** Write a short dialogue in your notebook between Shane and a friend at school in which Shane tells the story of the crocodile attack.

7

1 TURNING POINTS
4 Integrated Skills
Describing a significant event

1 Reading

Read and complete the text with these words.

> arrived became black carried hungry holiday light separate started took voted waited walked won

http://www.amazing-eventsinhistory.com

300 YEARS OF WAITING

On 27th April 1994 black people voted in South Africa's elections for the first time in 300 years. Before that date, there were laws to keep white and black people (1) _____ and only white people could vote for the national government.

'Today is a day like no other before it,' said Nelson Mandela, the leader and hero of the (2) _____ people's fight for freedom. The election (3) _____ place four years after he was freed after 27 years in prison. 'Voting in our first free and fair election has begun. Today marks the dawn of our freedom,' he said with a smile.

For three days black people (4) _____ patiently in queues at the polling stations. Some (5) _____ many miles to get there. The old and disabled (6) _____ in wheelchairs; some people (7) _____ sick family members in their arms. The queues (8) _____ very early in the morning before it was (9) _____ and many people waited all day. 'It was great, it was so easy,' said 86-year-old Johanas Sithole, who waited hours to vote in the black township of Alexandra. 'But I have to go home now because I'm (10) _____!'

Nearly 20 million people voted over the three-day election period; 16 million of them had never (11) _____ before. Nelson Mandela's ANC party (12) _____ 62.5% of the votes and Nelson Mandela (13) _____ the country's first black president.

April 27th is now a public (14) _____ in South Africa. It is called Freedom Day.

8

UNIT 1

2 Reading

Read the sentences and write *T* (true) or *F* (false). Correct the false sentences.

1. Before 1994 black people couldn't vote in South African government elections. ☐
2. Nearly two million black people voted in the 1994 election. ☐
3. White people couldn't vote in the 1994 election. ☐
4. Everyone voted on the same day. ☐
5. Only young people could go to the polling stations. ☐
6. Nelson Mandela's party won the 1994 election. ☐

3 Crossword

Complete the crossword.

Across →
1. A religious leader. (8)
4. Rosa Parks didn't give up ... seat. (3)
5. It's nice to hear a friend's ... on the phone. (5)
9. Something that happens. (5)
11. Appear to be. (4)
13. The shark ... off Bethany's arm. (3)
14. When Shane kicked the crocodile, it opened its ... (4)
15. If you feel this, your face goes red. (11)

Down ↓
1. Very unhappy. (9)
2. I'll ... forget the first time I saw a wolf. (5)
3. Dr Martin Luther King was one of the people who ... the bus boycott. (9)
6. Rob plays in a band ... Saturdays. (2)
7. Bethany saw the shark and then ... attacked her. (2)
8. Short for *examination*. (4)
10. Trousers made of denim. (5)
12. Have you ... seen a wolf? (4)

LEARNER INDEPENDENCE

Study plan

Make a study plan for next week. Use this example to help you.

> **Things to do before my English lessons**
> Finish the homework and remember to take my dictionary.
> **Reviewing my learning**
> Look back through Unit 1 and read all the texts again. Revise the phrasal verbs!
> **Grammar**
> Read the Language File for Unit 1.
> **Vocabulary**
> Make a word map for feelings.
>
>
>
> **Using my English**
> Phone Anita and have a five-minute conversation in English. Send an email in English to my friend in Iceland.

Extensive reading

Read *Owl Creek Bridge and Other Stories*. Imagine you are a film director making a film of one of the stories in the book. Which actors will you choose to play the main characters and why? Then compare your choices with another student.

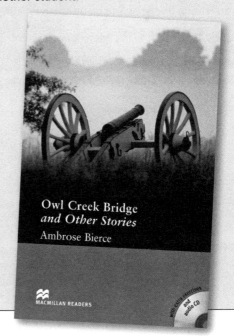

Eight short stories by the famous American journalist and writer, Ambrose Bierce. Learn about the American Civil War between the North and the South through stories like Peyton Farquhar's in *Owl Creek Bridge*. Peyton is about to be hanged on the bridge, but he tries to escape. Will he succeed? Read the story and find out!

1 TURNING POINTS
Inspiration EXTRA!

REVISION

LESSON 1

Present simple and present continuous: correct the sentences with mistakes.

1 Sophie and her friends ~~are meeting~~ in town at weekends.
   meet

2 She is talking about school, TV and boys with her friends.

3 Today she wears a hoodie, a denim skirt and boots.

4 She is looking forward to the school trip at half term.

5 Sophie and her friend Martha goes to the cinema once or twice a month.

6 Sophie reads a book called *The Host* at the moment.

7 She think most school lessons are interesting.

LESSON 2

Write questions and answers using the past simple.

1 Joni/go for a swim in the morning/afternoon
   Did Joni go for a swim in the morning?
   No, she didn't. She went for a swim in the afternoon.

2 Newquay/be a boring place/a great place

3 Joni/walk around the park/the harbour

4 Sara/write to her mother/her best friend

5 Joni's mother/come to see her/phone her

6 Sara's friends/be friendly/posh

LESSON 3

Write sentences using the past continuous + *when* + the past simple.

1 Bethany/surf with her friend Alana/the shark/attack
   Bethany was surfing with her friend Alana when the shark attacked.

2 Shane/help his father/he/decide to go for a swim

3 Shane/swim in the river/he/hear a splash behind him

4 Shane/answer his father/the crocodile/take his arm

5 Shane's father/wait for him/he/run back to the garden

LESSON 4

Write questions for these answers about Rosa Parks.

1 *Where did Rosa work?*
   In a department store.

2
   She sat in the first row of 'black' seats.

3
   To stand up so that a white man could sit down.

4
   They did what they were told.

5
   Because she was tired of giving in.

6
   They refused to use the buses for 381 days.

Spelling

Complete these words from Unit 1.

1 at___ack   2 b___ots   3 che___rful   4 col___ege   5 depres___ed
6 embar___as___ed   7 fe___ling   8 fre___dom   9 hap___y

Brainteaser

Why is an island like the letter T?

Answer on page 25.

UNIT 1

EXTENSION

LESSON 1

Write questions and answer them for yourself.

1 wear jeans today
   Are you wearing jeans today? Yes, I am./No, I'm not.

2 usually wear jeans to school
   Do you usually wear jeans to school?
   Yes, I do./No, I don't.

3 go to the cinema every week

4 worry about exams

5 look forward to the weekend

6 what kind of music/listen to

7 what/want to do today after school

LESSON 2

Write questions about yesterday and answer them for yourself.

1 what time/get up
   What time did you get up?
   I got up at seven o'clock.

2 what/have for breakfast

3 what/do after breakfast

4 who/talk to in the morning

5 when/have lunch

6 what/do in the evening

LESSON 3

Write sentences about what you were doing at these times last Saturday.

8am
At 8am, I was dreaming of surfing.

11am

1pm

5pm

8pm

11pm

LESSON 4

Use the notes you made in the interview with another student in exercise 5 on page 17 of the Student's Book to write about that student's significant event.

Web watch

Search for 'Bethany Hamilton' on the Internet and find out more about her life. Look up new words in the dictionary and make a *Brave people* section in your vocabulary notebook.

Spelling

The sound /i/ at the end of English words is usually written -y. But sometimes the same sound is written -ey or -ie.

Read and complete the words from Unit 1.

1 mon____   2 activit____   3 lonel____   4 journ____
5 mov____   6 biolog____   7 monk____   8 suddenl____
9 universit____   10 hock____

Brainteaser

What often falls but never gets hurt?

Answer on page 25.

1 Culture

WOMEN IN THE WORLD

Women in the press
People say that women have the same rights as men. They have the right to vote. They can have seats in parliament. They can even become heads of state. But they don't always have equal treatment in the press.

Female politicians
Journalists don't usually write stories about the private lives of politicians, unless those stories affect their work in some way. But for female politicians, this rule often doesn't apply. The way they look, how attractive or unattractive they are, their height, clothes and even their relationships are all the subject of numerous newspaper articles. Journalists frequently ask Australian Prime Minister Julia Gillard why she has never married. Male politicians don't have to put up with the constant commentary on their appearance and the endless personal questions that female Members of Parliament and political figures do.

Politicians' wives
The newspapers also pay a lot of attention to the way the politicians' wives look.

When Carla Bruni, wife of the French President Nicolas Sarkozy, visited the UK, the newspapers were full of stories criticising Sarah Brown, wife of the UK Prime Minister at the time. They said her clothes were boring and unfashionable when compared to Carla Bruni's. As former UK Prime Minister Tony Blair became more unpopular, the number of newspaper articles saying unpleasant things about the appearance of his wife, Cherie, increased.

During the 2010 election in the UK there were newspaper articles almost daily comparing the clothes of the party leaders' wives: Sarah Brown, Samantha Cameron and Miriam González Durántez, Nick Clegg's wife. When the United States' First Lady, Michelle Obama, wore a sleeveless dress to a political event, her choice of clothes inspired many newspaper articles, possibly more than her husband's political activities did.

Does it matter?
Is this important? Many people think it's fun or just another way for newspapers to fill their pages with things that people want to read, or that they are simply giving their readers entertainment. However, there is a more serious side to consider. Some readers could get the impression that women should not be taken seriously as politicians; that the only interesting thing about them is the way they look. The result of this may be that many intelligent women decide not to become politicians. After all, who would want a job in which their appearance was criticised day after day?

Some experts say that turning politics into a kind of soap opera means that people don't try to understand the important issues and problems of the day; it's much easier and more fun to read an article about what Samantha Cameron wore when she went to a royal wedding.

Culture

1 Reading

Read *Women in the world* and answer the questions.

Who ...
1. is married to Nick Clegg?
2. wore a sleeveless dress?
3. was compared to Sarah Brown?
4. went to a royal wedding?
5. visited the UK from France?
6. wore unfashionable clothes, according to the press?
7. doesn't have a husband?
8. write newspaper articles?
9. did the newspapers criticise when her husband was unpopular?
10. is married to Carla Bruni?

2 Reading

Read the text again and match the beginnings of the sentences with the endings.

1. Journalists don't usually
2. Newspaper readers
3. Newspapers were more interested
4. The message readers might get is
5. Newspapers don't usually comment on
6. The number of articles about Cherie Blair
7. Journalists ask Julia Gillard

a. in Michelle Obama's dress than in what her husband did.
b. increased as her husband became more unpopular.
c. write stories about the personal lives of male politicians.
d. the appearance and clothes of male politicians.
e. questions about her personal life.
f. find it easier to read about fashion than politics.
g. that women in politics aren't very important.

3 Vocabulary

Complete the sentences with these words.

> appearance   constant   criticise   entertainment   inspire
> journalist   press   put up with   soap opera   sleeveless

1. A .... is someone who writes articles for a newspaper.
2. To .... is to say something bad or unpleasant about someone.
3. A .... is a popular television drama.
4. Films, concerts and TV series are popular forms of ....
5. .... is the way someone or something looks.
6. A .... dress is one that has no sleeves.
7. Something which is .... happens all the time.
8. To .... something is to carry on even though it is unpleasant.
9. The .... are all the newspapers and magazines.
10. To .... something is to cause it to happen.

4 Writing

Write about a famous woman in your country. What kind of stories do the newspapers write about her?

2 ARTS
1 You can't help laughing

1 Reading
Read the descriptions of three films and match them with the pictures.

1 ☐
This film tells the extraordinary story of Bertie, the second son of Britain's King George V, who hates speaking in public because he has a stammer. When he has to become king instead of his brother, it becomes even more important that he learns to speak clearly. Bertie's wife starts looking for a doctor who can help him. It's a film about history, but the actors and director are very good at keeping viewers interested in the story.

2 ☐
Kim Matthews is a champion skateboarder, but now she has to give up skateboarding and get a job to help her father. She ends up working in the Alps, cooking and cleaning for the posh people who go there to ski. That's where she discovers that she loves snowboarding. Can she succeed in becoming a champion again?

3 ☐
Dragons keep attacking the people on the Island of Berk. A boy called Hiccup dreams of joining the men in their battle with the dragons, but his father says no. Hiccup succeeds in catching a dragon, but he finds that he doesn't want to kill it. The two become friends and find a way to get the men and the dragons to stop fighting.

2 Reading
Read the sentences and write *T* (true) or *F* (false). Correct the false sentences.

1 The men of Berk start killing dragons to protect their island. ☐

2 Hiccup enjoyed killing the dragon he caught. ☐

3 Hiccup and his dragon friend don't succeed in stopping the fighting. ☐

4 Kim Matthews loves skateboarding and snowboarding. ☐

5 Bertie isn't good at speaking in public. ☐

6 The director doesn't know how to keep viewers' attention. ☐

3 Verb/Preposition + gerund
Complete with the gerund form of these verbs.

| become cry play talk think watch |

1 It was a really scary film, and I can't stop .... about it.
2 Sean Connery was brilliant at .... James Bond.
3 Lots of young people dream of .... famous film stars.
4 Aren't you fed up with .... romantic films every weekend?
5 I can't help .... when I'm watching sad films.
6 Shh! Stop .... – the film is starting!

4 *so/nor* + auxiliary verbs
Complete with *so/nor* + auxiliary verbs.

1 Rob likes horror films and *so does* Sophie.
2 Beth isn't keen on musicals and .... I.
3 Dave can play the guitar and .... Paul.
4 You're scared of spiders and .... I.
5 I'm interested in politics and .... my friends.
6 Emily doesn't mind cooking and .... Alex.

5 Verb + gerund, so/nor + auxiliary verbs

What do Emily and Alex like doing at the weekend? Look at the chart and complete the dialogue.

love ✔ don't mind **OK** can't stand ✘

	Emily	Alex
go to parties	✔	✔
swim in the sea	OK	✘
watch DVDs	✔	✔
play computer games	OK	OK
iron my clothes	✘	✘
buy clothes	OK	✔

EMILY I (**1**) _love going to_ parties.
ALEX (**2**) _____ .
EMILY I (**3**) _____ in the sea.
ALEX Don't you? I (**4**) _____ in seawater.
EMILY What about DVDs? I (**5**) _____ DVDs at weekends.
ALEX (**6**) _____ .
EMILY And I (**7**) _____ computer games.
ALEX (**8**) _____ .
EMILY As for housework, I (**9**) _____ my clothes.
ALEX (**10**) _____ .
EMILY But I (**11**) _____ clothes.
ALEX I (**12**) _____ Let's go shopping!

6 Vocabulary

Complete with these prepositions.

about at for in (x2) of (x2) on with

1 How _____ going to the cinema?
2 Sometimes I dream _____ becoming a famous Hollywood star.
3 Are you interested _____ watching a documentary?
4 I'm keen _____ horror films.
5 I'm not scared _____ anything.
6 Hollywood is famous _____ making movies.
7 He falls _____ love _____ Bella.
8 My brother is very good _____ acting.

7 Vocabulary

Find 12 adjectives you can use to give your opinion in the word square.

A	W	F	U	L	T	B	A	D	B	C	U	T
E	L	U	P	T	A	S	C	A	R	Y	D	H
X	I	N	T	E	R	E	S	T	I	N	G	R
C	H	N	M	R	D	O	V	C	L	P	O	I
I	A	Y	Q	R	P	S	I	L	L	Y	O	L
T	E	M	R	I	D	I	C	N	I	G	D	L
I	K	N	T	B	I	B	S	R	A	N	H	I
N	F	G	I	L	B	O	R	I	N	G	C	N
G	E	X	C	E	L	L	E	N	T	Y	W	G

8 Pronunciation

Complete the chart with these words.

| ~~attack~~ avoid drama enjoy horror kidnap |
| pirate planet protect remove rescue succeed |

▪ ▪	▪ ▪
attack	

9 Pronunciation

Do they rhyme (✔) or not (✘)?

1	laugh	half	✔
2	curse	worse	☐
3	blood	good	☐
4	lose	close	☐
5	scary	diary	☐
6	danger	stranger	☐
7	scared	hard	☐
8	dream	seem	☐

Extension Look at the chart in exercise 5 again and write six sentences in your notebook about yourself and somebody in your family.

I love going to parties and so does my sister.

2 ARTS
Promise to work together

1 Reading

Read the dialogue between two *Star School* contestants.

NICK   What do you hope to learn at *Star School*?
LORNA I want to develop my voice – I'd like to sing like Joss Stone.
NICK   So you want to sing the blues.
LORNA That's right. And I asked Adam to teach me ballet. What about you?
NICK   Adam says he can teach us to dance, and I promise to try. But I refuse to do ballet – I've got two left feet when it comes to ballet!
LORNA I don't believe you! Do you expect to win the competition?
NICK   No, but I hope to spend a few weeks here.

Now complete these sentences with *Nick* or *Lorna*.

1 .... wants to sing the blues.
2 .... doesn't want to do ballet.
3 .... promises to try in the dance classes.
4 .... doesn't expect to win the competition.
5 .... hopes to sing like Joss Stone.
6 .... is keen to learn ballet.

2 Verb + infinitive

Rewrite the sentences using the words in capitals.

1 NICK   I won't do ballet.   REFUSE
   He refuses to do ballet.
2 LORNA I'd like to learn ballet.   WANT
   ....
3 JESS   I'll help everyone to sing better.   PROMISE
   ....
4 ADAM   I can teach the contestants breakdancing.   OFFER
   ....
5 TONY   I want everyone to obey the rules.   ASK
   ....
6 NICK   OK, I'll try to dance.   AGREE
   ....

3 Verb (+ object) + infinitive

Complete with the infinitive of the verb. Include the correct object pronoun (*it, me, you*) where necessary.

Do you want (**1**) .... (become) successful performers? Then I'd like (**2**) .... (listen) carefully. We can teach (**3**) .... (sing) and dance, but you must promise (**4**) .... (work) hard. Don't expect (**5**) .... (be) easy and don't pretend (**6**) .... (know) everything. You can learn (**7**) .... (do) lots of new things here, so don't refuse (**8**) .... (try). We can help (**9**) .... (develop) your talents, and I hope you manage (**10**) .... (work) with each other. All our contestants hope (**11**) .... (win), but there can only be one winner. Right, any questions? Is there anything you want (**12**) .... (explain)?

4 Verb + infinitive or gerund

Complete with the correct form of the verbs.

1 Most contestants succeed in .... (write) songs.
2 Why did you decide .... (give up) salsa?
3 Promise .... (tell) me if you have any problems.
4 Do you enjoy .... (listen) to classical music?
5 Nick isn't very good at .... (dance).
6 Lorna seems .... (be) a very confident performer.
7 Oh dear, I keep .... (forget) the words!
8 Adam told us .... (try) new ideas.

16

5 Vocabulary

Complete with these prepositions.

| ~~at~~ | by | for | in | like | of | on | with |

Star School is a new reality TV show. Ten contestants learn to sing and write songs (**1**) ___at___ the school. They perform their songs (**2**) _____ TV – but not everyone (**3**) _____ the show can sing (**4**) _____ a star. Viewers vote (**5**) _____ their favourite performer (**6**) _____ phone, and the contestant (**7**) _____ the highest number (**8**) _____ votes is the winner.

6 Crossword

Complete the crossword and find this word ↓.

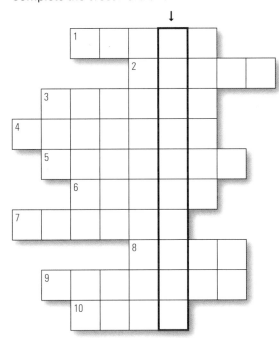

1. You can't sing without this!
2. Someone who trains people.
3. A special ability.
4. Noun formed from *real*.
5. Noun formed from *succeed*.
6. Popular Latin-American dance.
7. Classical dance.
8. A type of dance that is also a type of music.
9. Someone you work together with.
10. Someone who writes poems.

7 Vocabulary

Compare the words in list A with the words in list B. Write *S* if they have almost the same meaning, *O* if they are opposites, and *G* if A is more general than B.

	A	B	
1	dance	ballet	*G*
2	coach	teacher	
3	simple	difficult	
4	teach	learn	
5	music	jazz	
6	hope	want	
7	agree	refuse	
8	writer	poet	
9	perform	act	
10	enjoy	like	

8 Vocabulary

Match the words in list A with the words in list B and write six compound nouns.

	A	B		
1	ball	show	1	*ballroom*
2	break	letter	2	
3	song	dancing	3	
4	dance	room	4	
5	thank-you	routine	5	
6	talent	writing	6	

9 Pronunciation

Write the number of syllables and mark the stressed syllable.

contestant _3_   develop _____   experiment _____

important _____   reality _____   songwriting _____

hopeful _____   questionnaire _____

> **Extension** Imagine you are a contestant on *Star School*. Write four sentences in your notebook about what you want to do and what you don't want to do on the show.

ARTS

3 Books are left in public places

1 Reading

Read the text and answer the questions below.

How a book is made

What happens after a writer finishes a book and sends it to a publisher? At this stage, the book is called a manuscript. The manuscript is read by the editor and mistakes are corrected. Then the manuscript is given to the designer. The text is laid out on pages by the designer, pictures are drawn by artists, and photographs are chosen by picture researchers. When everything is ready, the pages of the book are made into electronic files and sent to the printer. The pages are printed on large sheets of paper, and then they are folded. Finally, the pages are put together to make a book.

1 Who reads the manuscript and corrects the mistakes?

2 Who gets the manuscript after the editor?

3 What does the designer do to the text?

4 What do picture researchers do?

5 What happens after the pages are folded?

2 Past participles

Complete the chart. Write *R* for regular verbs or *I* for irregular verbs.

Infinitive	Past participle	
buy	*bought*	*I*
drink		
find		
grow		
invite		
leave		
make		
produce		
publish		
sell		
take		
teach		
visit		

3 Present simple passive

Write questions and answer them using these countries.

Antarctica   France   Italy   Japan   ~~Kenya~~   Switzerland

1 coffee/grow?

   Where is coffee grown?
   It's grown in Kenya.

2 French, German and Italian/speak?

3 pasta/eat?

4 kimonos/wear?

5 champagne/make?

6 penguins/find?

UNIT 2

4 Present simple passive

Write sentences using *by* + agent. Use these phrases.

> a school band   a voice coach   film directors
> publishers   ~~reporters~~   artists

1 newspaper stories/write
   Newspaper stories are written by reporters.

2 singing/teach

3 this music/perform

4 pictures/draw

5 movies/make

6 books/produce

5 Present simple passive

Dan Deacon is a famous rock musician, and his manager organises everything for him. Write sentences using the present simple passive.

1 He doesn't arrange his concerts.

His concerts are arranged for him.

2 He doesn't choose his clothes.

3 He doesn't carry his bags.

4 He doesn't book his flights.

5 He doesn't buy his food.

6 He doesn't clean his flat.

7 He doesn't pay his hotel bills.

8 He doesn't plan his life.

6 Vocabulary

Complete the sentences with these verbs to make phrasal verbs with *up*.

> give   ~~grow~~   look   pick   set   stand   turn

1 My brother wants to be a pilot when he _grows_ up.

2 The students .... up when the teacher entered the room.

3 We expect lots of people to .... up at the football match.

4 Keep trying – don't .... up!

5 You can't .... up a business without money.

6 Try to guess the meaning of a word before you .... it up.

7 Vocabulary

Match these words with their definitions.

> borrow   character   globe   increasing   public   unique

1 world, or something round like a ball

2 opposite of *lend*

3 for everyone to use

4 person in a book

5 different from anything else

6 getting bigger

8 Pronunciation

Write the number of syllables and mark the stressed syllable.

character *3*   comment ......   enthusiastic ......

increasing ......   invitation ......   library ......

paperback ......   register ......   unique ......   virtual ......

9 Pronunciation

Do they rhyme (✔) or not (✘)?

1 cover	over	✘
2 goal	whole	☐
3 table	label	☐
4 try	buy	☐
5 turn	learn	☐
6 grown	town	☐

> **Extension** What was the last film you enjoyed? Write four sentences in your notebook about it for a film review website.

2.4 ARTS

Integrated Skills

Describing a picture

1 Reading

Read and match the texts with two of the paintings. Title the texts, and then complete them with these phrases.

a   which is not healthy at all
b   which is absurd
c   who's lying on the wall
d   who's wearing a black coat over a white shirt and red tie
e   who painted this picture
f   which is against the wall
g   which means a lot to me

A ....

This is one of my favourite paintings. The man (**1**) .... looks like an office worker. He's wearing a dark jacket and trousers, and black shoes. He has an umbrella, (**2**) .... , and a briefcase. The man is smoking a cigarette, (**3**) .... Behind the wall there's a tall church on the left, and in the middle there are two factory chimneys. This picture makes me feel happy, because it's funny. It also tells me 'Take a break from work – stop and think about life.'

B ....

This is a picture (**4**) .... It shows a man in a black bowler hat (**5**) .... He looks very smart, like a businessman. The picture is painted in a very realistic way, except that there's a big green apple in front of the man's face, (**6**) .... I want to know what the man's face looks like, but the man can't see very much either. He's standing in front of a wall and there are dark clouds above the sea behind him. The artist (**7**) .... said 'Everything we see hides another thing, we always want to see what is hidden by what we see.' The painting makes me feel a bit frustrated. Life doesn't make sense sometimes, but we can't know everything.

The Son of Man by René Magritte

Man Lying on a Wall by L.S. Lowry

20

2 Writing

Write a short description of the third painting, and say how it makes you feel.

3 Crossword

Complete the crossword.

Across →
1 Very, very good. (9)
6 Are you good ... spelling? (2)
8 A film or play which has lots of songs. (7)
9 Books are ... of paper. (4)
10 'Do you like garlic?' – 'No, I can't ... it.' (5)
12 A flying insect with a black and yellow body. (3)
13 I'm looking forward ... the holidays. (2)
14 Plural of *me*. (2)
17 You can ... the suffixes *-ful* and *-less* to *pain*, *hope*, and *care*. (3)
19 Something which you hide from other people. (6)
20 Something which belongs to you is your ... (3)
21 Bella Swan is... love with a vampire! (2)
22 Opposite of *bored*. (10)

Down ↓
1 Very, very large. (8)
2 A film or play which makes you laugh. (6)
3 Opposite of *found*. (4)
4 Very happy and enthusiastic. (7)
5 When you can do something very well, you have a ... for it. (6)
10 You sit on this, in the cinema, for example. (4)
11 Lots of trees are cut ... to make paper. (4)
15 Past participle of *see*. (4)
16 When something is ..., you don't pay for it. (4)
18 I ... mind watching documentaries – I quite like them. (4)
21 Who ... this book written by? (2)

LEARNER INDEPENDENCE

Pronunciation

It's useful to understand phonemic script because it will help you to pronounce English words correctly. Write these words, which are all in texts 1–3 on pages 28–29 of the Student's Book. You can use the Pronunciation Guide on page 127 of the Student's Book to help you.

1 /ˈbækɡraʊnd/
2 /ˈdefɪnətli/
3 /ɪkˈspreʃən/
4 /rɪəˈlɪstɪk/
5 /wɔː/
6 /ˈpeɪnfəl/
7 /ˈɪmɪdʒ/
8 /ˈfeɪvərɪt/

Now check your answers in the Word List at the back of the Student's Book.

Extensive reading

Read *Casino Royale*. How do you think Bond feels at the end of the story?

Now imagine you are James Bond, and write your report for the British Secret Service about Vesper's role in the story.

Casino Royale is Ian Fleming's first novel about James Bond, the handsome British secret agent 007. Bond goes to the Casino at Royale-les-Eaux in France to destroy Le Chiffre, a dangerous Russian agent, by winning all his money. Bond's new assistant is a very beautiful woman called Vesper Lynd. He soon starts to like Vesper – very much – and wants to spend more time with her. But Le Chiffre has other plans ...

2 ARTS
Inspiration EXTRA!

REVISION

LESSON 1

Complete with the gerund form of these verbs.

| fly | forget | get | go | learn | make | stand | swim |

1 Are you interested in _____ Japanese?
2 I'm not keen on _____ in cold water.
3 Lots of people are scared of _____.
4 There aren't enough chairs, but we don't mind _____.
5 I always avoid _____ out when it's raining.
6 What's the matter with him? He keeps _____ important things.
7 Let's start _____ a shopping list.
8 People who do dangerous sports risk _____ hurt.

LESSON 2

Here are Nick's answers to the *Truth Questionnaire* on page 25 of the Student's Book. Write a paragraph about him.

1 Yes.
2 Windsurfing.
3 To laugh at my jokes.
4 Olives.
5 Cucumber.
6 To wash the car.
7 To play the guitar.
8 To travel.

He promises to tell the truth. He wants to learn

LESSON 3

Complete with the verbs in the present simple passive.

Tea (1) _____ (grow) in many Asian countries. The green leaves (2) _____ (pick) by hand and they (3) _____ (take) to the factory. The leaves (4) _____ (lay) out until they become drier, and then they (5) _____ (pass) between rollers. The rolled tea (6) _____ (lay) out again, and then the leaves (7) _____ (dry) in hot air until they turn black. Finally, the black tea (8) _____ (put) into boxes and it (9) _____ (sell) all over the world.

LESSON 4

Complete the definitions with *which* or *who* and these phrases.

| doesn't have a hard cover   takes part in a competition |
| describes real people and events   teaches you a skill |
| is usually grown in water   steals things from ships at sea |
| which is at the front   has books you can read or borrow |

1 A documentary is a film _____
2 The foreground is the part of a picture _____
3 A coach is a person _____
4 A contestant is someone _____
5 A library is a place _____
6 A paperback is a book _____
7 A pirate is a person _____
8 Rice is a grain _____

Spelling

Complete these words from Unit 2 with the silent letters.

1 balle___ 2 bou___t 3 fi___t 4 fr___end 5 g___ard
6 han___kerchief 7 i___land 8 throu___

Brainteaser

What has roads and rivers, but no cars or boats?
Answer on page 25.

22

UNIT 2

EXTENSION

LESSON 1

Complete the sentences for yourself using the gerund.

1 I can't stand
2 I really want to give up
3 I don't feel like
4 I never get fed up with
5 Yesterday I succeeded in
6 I'm quite good at
7 I'd like to start
8 I couldn't help

LESSON 2

Complete the sentences for yourself using the infinitive.

1 I'd really like
2 At the weekend I hope
3 Yesterday I agreed
4 Today our teacher taught us
5 My parents expect me
6 I usually help
7 I don't want
8 I sometimes pretend

LESSON 3

Complete with the verbs in the present simple active or passive.

The news reports from foreign countries which you (1) _____ (see) on television (2) _____ (film) with a digital video camera. The pictures and the sounds (3) _____ (turn) into electric signals by the camera, and these signals (4) _____ (send) by a digital phone to a satellite. The satellite (5) _____ (send) the signals to the TV station. At the TV station the news reports (6) _____ (put) into programmes and (7) _____ (carry) to you by cable, satellite or television transmitter. When you (8) _____ (turn) on the TV, the digital signals (9) _____ (become) pictures and sounds again.

LESSON 4

Write in your notebook a short description of this photo, and say how it makes you feel.

Comic critic

Web watch

Search for 'Forget it, Forget Me' by Roy Lichtenstein on the Internet and find out more about the painting and the artist. Look up new words in the dictionary and make an *Art and artists* section in your vocabulary notebook.

Spelling

Some English words have the same sound but different spellings, for example /ðeə/ = *their* and *there*. These words are called homophones.

Write the homophones of these words. All the homophones are in Unit 2.

1 /bɔːd/ board
2 /baɪ/ bye
3 /raɪt/ write
4 /aʊə/ hour
5 /nəʊ/ no
6 /piːs/ piece
7 /siː/ see
8 /sʌn/ son

Brainteaser

What travels at the speed of sound, but has no legs, wings or engines?

Answer on page 25.

REVIEW
UNITS 1–2

1 Read and complete. For each number 1–15, choose word or phrase A, B, C or D.

TEENAGE KICKS

The taxi was taking me and a newspaper reporter to the opening night of Paul McCartney's European Tour in the Spanish town of Gijón. We (**1**) _____ an advertisement for tonight's show with a picture of a middle-aged man who (**2**) _____ a guitar. 'So is that what Paul McCartney looks like?' I asked. The reporter frowned and looked at me. Even the taxi driver, who as far as I knew, (**3**) _____ any English, was looking at me in his mirror.

It didn't seem right to me – how can I know what Paul McCartney (**4**) _____ like? I'm 17 years old. The last time he had a top ten hit, in 1987, I wasn't even born. It was all the reporter's idea. I'm not really interested in (**5**) _____ to 'old' music and know very little about it. But I am keen on (**6**) _____ to my local clubs to see ska and punk bands. I love listening to Muse, Faithless and Massive Attack. So when the reporter told me the names of the bands we were seeing – McCartney, Diana Ross, Brian Wilson, the Who and Kraftwerk – I didn't know them. I thought Kraftwerk were a cheap German airline. The reporter wanted me (**7**) _____ the bands and give a teenager's opinion of them.

The first gig was Brian Wilson – he was in the Beach Boys in the 60s and wrote their songs. It was like classical music. It sounded nothing at all like the music that (**8**) _____ today. A few days later, the reporter rang me at school on my mobile in the lunch break. The next gig was Diana Ross. Years of half-listening to songs of hers like *Baby Love* which (**9**) _____ in shopping centres made her music familiar to me. Brian Wilson stared at the audience like a kind of reptile, but Diana walked out into the audience and at one point hugged them!

Kraftwerk were quite different. For a start, in the audience there were ten men in leather for every one woman. There were no guitars or drums, just four middle-aged men in black suits singing songs like *I'm the operator with my pocket calculator*. Both the reporter and I (**10**) _____ they were fantastic. After a month of exam revision, the next band was the Who. Good name, I thought. But their music blew me away. It was incredibly powerful rock – no chance of falling asleep there. Now I could understand why parents make their children (**11**) _____ to *My Generation*.

And finally McCartney. He started with a band and some old Beatles' songs. It sounded just like a middle-of-the-road English rock band. I wanted him (**12**) _____ on his own. But then he did and things got much better. He began with *Back in the USSR* and ended with *Helter Skelter*. He said he wanted us (**13**) _____ along with *Hey Jude* and *Yellow Submarine* and we did. It was great and it was 1.30 before he (**14**) _____ .

So what did I learn? I still think music from the 60s and 70s sounds like an early version of the music which (**15**) _____ today. And although I enjoyed some of the live concerts, I get bored by listening to their albums afterwards.

1	**A** pass	**B** passing	**C** are passing	**D** passed
2	**A** plays	**B** played	**C** was playing	**D** were playing
3	**A** wasn't speaking	**B** didn't speak	**C** isn't speaking	**D** doesn't speak
4	**A** looks	**B** is looking	**C** looked	**D** was looking
5	**A** listen	**B** to listen	**C** listening	**D** was listening
6	**A** go	**B** going	**C** to go	**D** be going
7	**A** hear	**B** to hear	**C** hears	**D** hearing
8	**A** is played	**B** is playing	**C** plays	**D** play
9	**A** play	**B** are playing	**C** played	**D** are played
10	**A** think	**B** are thinking	**C** thought	**D** were thinking
11	**A** listen	**B** to listen	**C** listening	**D** listens
12	**A** play	**B** to play	**C** playing	**D** plays
13	**A** sing	**B** to sing	**C** singing	**D** sings
14	**A** finishes	**B** is finishing	**C** finished	**D** was finishing
15	**A** makes	**B** is making	**C** is made	**D** was making

2 Complete with the correct form of the word in capitals.

1 The class had a good _____ about language learning. DISCUSS
2 I know something's wrong – you look so _____. WORRY
3 Until he met her he didn't know what real _____ was. HAPPY
4 She hopes to change things so she wants to be a _____. POLITICS
5 It's a good idea but will it work? Is it _____? REAL
6 She passed all her exams _____. SUCCESS

3 Complete the second sentence so that it means the same as the first sentence. Use the word in bold without changing it.

1 I can't wait to see my parents again. **forward**
   I'm really _____
2 'I'm sorry I was angry,' she said. **being**
   She apologised _____
3 Nothing went right from the beginning. **wrong**
   It _____
4 She was waiting for the bus and then she saw Tina. **when**
   She _____
5 Surfing is something most people can do. **good**
   Most people _____
6 Online booksellers sell more and more books. **by**
   More and more books _____

4 Find the odd word.

1 ocean   water   wave   (beach)
2 depressed   excited   lonely   miserable
3 cheerful   frightened   scared   terrified
4 kick   hit   punch   shout
5 comedy   documentary   musical   paperback
6 ballet   breakdancing   coach   salsa
7 bench   chair   seat   stage
8 boring   brilliant   excellent   interesting

Answers to Brainteasers

UNIT 1
Revision Because it's in the middle of water (WA**T**ER).
Extension rain or snow

UNIT 2
Revision a map
Extension your voice

LEARNER INDEPENDENCE
SELF ASSESSMENT

Vocabulary

1 Draw this chart in your notebook. How many words can you write in each category?

More than 10? Good!   *More than 12?* Very good!
More than 15? Excellent!

Music and dance	
Films	
Feelings	

2 Put the words in order to make expressions from the phrasebooks in Lesson 4 in Units 1 and 2.

1 can't wait I
   I can't wait.
2 believe I couldn't it
   _____
3 wrong went everything
   _____
4 never the time first I'll forget I
   _____
5 why it not try
   _____
6 promise truth to do tell you the
   _____
7 can't laughing you help
   _____
8 me it of reminds
   _____

Check your answers.
8/8 Excellent!   *6/8* Very good!   *4/8* Try again!

My learning diary
In Units 1 and 2:

My favourite topic is _____

My favourite picture is _____

The three lessons I like most are _____

My favourite activity or exercise is _____

Something I don't understand is _____

Something I want to learn more about is _____

OPINIONS

There could be tens of billions of planets

1 Reading

Read the dialogue and complete it with *must* or *can't*.

DAVE   Look at this amazing photo. It says here that a Mr R Herring took it last night in the sky over a field near his house. Do you think it's a UFO, a spaceship from another planet?

LINDA Of course not! Don't be silly, Dave. It (**1**) .... be from another planet. There are no spaceships from other planets!

DAVE   How do you know? There are billions of planets out there and at least one of them (**2**) .... be like Earth. This (**3**) .... be the only planet in the universe which can support life.

LINDA You (**4**) .... be serious! Do you really believe that there are little green men from Mars in spaceships who fly down to look at us?

DAVE   They may not be little, they may not be men and they may not be from Mars, but yes, I think it's possible that we are visited by people from other planets.

LINDA You (**5**) .... be joking!

DAVE   Well, what do you think this photo shows?

LINDA It (**6**) .... be a plane.

DAVE   It (**7**) .... be a plane. It says here that it moved very quickly from left to right and back again and then it disappeared. Planes don't do that!

LINDA Well, it (**8**) .... be a real photograph, then. It (**9**) .... be a trick of some kind. What's the date of the newspaper? It's not 1st April, is it?

DAVE   You're right. I (**10**) .... be stupid!

LINDA You said it!

2 *must* or *can't*

Complete these dialogues with *must* or *can't*.

1

A Which two planets are hotter than Earth?

B It .... be Mercury and Venus because they're nearer to the Sun.

2

A And which planet is hotter, Mercury or Venus?

B It .... be Mercury. Again, because it's nearer the Sun.

A No, actually, you're wrong. Venus is hotter because it has an atmosphere which keeps the heat in.

3

A Is Earth the biggest planet?

B No, it .... be. It's much smaller than Jupiter or Saturn. I think the biggest planet .... be Jupiter.

4

A Which planet is furthest away from the Sun, Jupiter or Neptune?

B It .... be Jupiter because it is next to Mars so it .... be Neptune.

5

A Is Neptune the coldest planet, then?

B Yes, I think it .... be.

26

3 could/may/might, must and can't

Ann and Lucy are camping in a field. Complete the dialogue with *could/may/might, must* or *can't*.

LUCY Ann, Ann, wake up!
ANN What's the matter? It (**1**) _____ be time to get up. It's still dark.
LUCY I heard a strange noise. There's someone or something outside the tent. Can't you hear it?
ANN I can't hear anything. You (**2**) _____ be dreaming. Go back to sleep!
LUCY I'm sure I heard something. I suppose it (**3**) _____ be a cow or sheep, but there weren't any animals in the field when we put up the tent. I'm going outside to check. Ann, look, there's a light over there by the trees.
ANN There (**4**) _____ be! We're in the middle of the country and there aren't any buildings in sight.
LUCY Well, what's that, then?
ANN I don't know! It (**5**) _____ be a car or a motorbike or something like that.
LUCY But the road's over there on the other side. And can you hear a car or a motorbike?
ANN No, but what else (**6**) _____ it be?
LUCY Strange noises and lights ... Well, it (**7**) _____ be visitors from another planet.
ANN No, it (**8**) _____. There is no life on other planets! It's probably the farmer. He (**9**) _____ be checking his cows.
LUCY Yes, but what if it isn't?

4 Vocabulary

Complete with these words.

| astronomers | atmosphere | gravity | light year |
| orbit | star | solar system | surface |

1 The Sun isn't a planet, it is a *star*.
2 Our Sun and its eight planets are called the _____.
3 Scientists think there may be water on the _____ of Gliese 581 g.
4 _____ is the power that pulls things towards the centre of the Earth.
5 Eight planets _____ the Sun.
6 Planets without an _____ can't support life.
7 _____ have discovered a planet similar to Earth.
8 A _____ is the distance that light can travel in one year.

5 Crossword

Complete the crossword with words about the universe and find this word ↓.

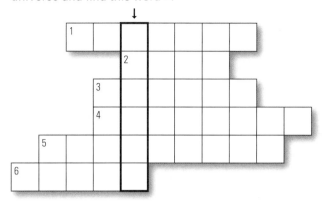

1 The eighth planet from the Sun.
2 There may be ... on other planets.
3 An enormous group of stars and planets.
4 Space and everything that exists in it.
5 Astronomers use one to look at the stars.
6 A machine which can do things on its own; it sometimes looks like a human.

6 Vocabulary

The same letter is missing in each line. Write the complete words.

1 roky   roket   Merury
2 alaxy   ravity   reions
3 liuid   uarter   uestion
4 suface   univese   obit
5 telecope   solar sytem   tar
6 sientists   acording   louds

7 Pronunciation

Do they rhyme (✔) or not (✘)?

1 snow   now   ✘
2 cloud   could   ☐
3 might   light   ☐
4 billion trillion ☐
5 water   quarter   ☐
6 place   plays   ☐

Extension Make another crossword like the one in exercise 5 using a different word in the centre. Write definitions for your words and ask another student to solve the crossword.

3 OPINIONS

2 When can you drive a car?

16 - the magic number!

In the UK, 16 is the age when you can do lots of things for the first time. You can't order your own passport until you are 16, and you have to be 16 to change your name. You don't have to be 16 to be a babysitter, but some people think that babysitters shouldn't be younger than 16. You can ride a moped (a motorbike with a small engine which cannot go faster than 50km an hour) when you're 16, but you have to wait until you're 17 before you can ride a 'real' motorbike or drive a car. You don't have to be any special age to ride a bicycle. And being 16 makes no difference when you go to the cinema – you can see a '15' film when you are 15, but you have to be 18 to see an '18' film.

1 Reading

Read the text. Then read the sentences and write T (true) or F (false).

In the UK ...

1 you can't order your own passport if you're under 16.
2 you can change your name if you're 16.
3 you can't be a babysitter until you're 16.
4 you can ride a moped if you're under 16.
5 you can ride a real motorbike when you're 17.
6 you can drive a car when you are 16.
7 you have to be 15 to ride a bicycle.
8 you have to be 16 to go to the cinema.

2 mustn't and don't have to

Complete these UK laws with *mustn't* or *don't have to*.

1 You _mustn't_ ride a motorbike before you're 17.
2 You _____ be 16 to see a '15' film.
3 You _____ buy fireworks if you're under 18.
4 You _____ be any special age to put money in a bank.
5 You _____ ride a moped if you're under 16.
6 You _____ be 21 to change your name.
7 You _____ go to an '18' film when you're 16.
8 You _____ be any special age to watch TV.

3 must, mustn't/can't and have to

Rewrite these strange US laws using the correct form of the verb.

1 In Denver, Colorado, it's illegal for your neighbour to borrow your vacuum cleaner. (must)

   In Denver, Colorado, your neighbour mustn't borrow your vacuum cleaner.

2 You aren't allowed to go fishing in your pyjamas in Chicago. (can)

3 In Ohio pets must have lights on their tails at night. (have to)

4 It's against the law to carry an ice cream in your pocket in Lexington, Kentucky. (can)

5 It's forbidden to wash two babies in the same bath at the same time in California. (must)

6 It's illegal to walk backwards after dark in Devon, Connecticut. (can)

7 In Utah you aren't allowed to go fishing on a horse. (must)

8 Men must wear a matching jacket and trousers in Carmel, New York State. (have to)

4 Reflexive pronouns

Complete with the correct reflexive pronoun.

1 We can see ___ourselves___ in the mirror.
2 She doesn't enjoy going on holiday by _____.
3 He cuts his hair _____.
4 They looked after _____ when their mother was away.
5 I cooked the meal _____.
6 Relax and make _____ at home.
7 It's illegal – I don't want to get _____ arrested.
8 My cat washes _____ all day.

5 Vocabulary

Write the opposites.

1 fall asleep
2 legal
3 allowed
4 carelessly
5 sell
6 full-time

6 Vocabulary

Match the verbs in list A with the words and phrases in list B. Then write the phrases.

	A	B		
1	break	in an election	1	*break a law*
2	come	a law	2	
3	keep	time	3	
4	leave	a secret	4	
5	get	up with an idea	5	
6	cross	school	6	
7	vote	the road	7	
8	spend	married	8	

7 Vocabulary

Match the words in list A with the words in list B and write six compound nouns.

	A	B		
1	lottery	square	1	*lottery ticket*
2	part-time	ticket	2	
3	school-leaving	holiday	3	
4	summer	licence	4	
5	town	age	5	
6	TV	job	6	

8 Pronunciation

Complete the chart with these words.

arrested carefully continent election forbidden holiday
illegal lottery motorbike permission possible reflexive

■ ■ ■	■ ■ ■
	arrested

Extension In your notebook, rewrite the false sentences in exercise 1 to make them true.

3 OPINIONS

3 You should calm down!

1 Reading

Monica is starting at a new school. Read the advice a friend gave her. Is it good advice or bad advice? Write *G* (good) or *B* (bad).

1 You shouldn't get there early on the first day. ☐
2 You should make sure your name is on all your things. ☐
3 You should stay up late the night before. ☐
4 You should expect to make lots of new friends at once. ☐
5 You shouldn't try to remember people's names. ☐
6 You shouldn't tell everyone that your last school was better. ☐
7 You shouldn't panic when everything seems strange. ☐
8 You shouldn't listen to your parents' advice. ☐

Now rewrite the bad advice in your notebook to make it good advice.

2 *ought to* and *shouldn't*

Look at the pictures on the right and give advice using these phrases.

You ought to ...
talk to new students at your school
calm down and take it easy
concentrate on what you're doing
~~choose what to leave behind~~
stay awake at school
queue up like everyone else

You shouldn't ...
ignore students who don't know anyone
fall asleep in class
lose your temper
push in front of people
~~take so many clothes with you~~
try to do two things at the same time

1 *You ought to choose what to leave behind.*
   You shouldn't take so many clothes with you.

2

3

4

5

6

3 should/ought to, shouldn't and had better (not)

Rewrite the sentences using the correct form of the verb or phrase.

1 You should tell the teacher if other students bully you. (ought)

2 We ought to hurry or we'll be late. (had better)

3 It's important to keep a friend's secret. (should)

4 It's wrong to cheat in exams. (should)

5 You shouldn't forget your dictionary today. (had better)

4 Adjective + infinitive

Complete with an adjective and an infinitive.

Adjectives
~~difficult~~   good   normal   possible   rude   wrong

Infinitives
bully   feel   forget   ~~hear~~   learn   point

1 It was *difficult to hear* what she was saying because of the noise.

2 In the UK, it's _____ your finger at people.

3 It's _____ new words before you go to sleep because you remember them the next day.

4 He knew that he was _____ the new student and he apologised.

5 It's _____ tired after a very long day.

6 It's _____ everything you learnt when you're nervous in an exam.

5 Vocabulary

Match the verbs in list A with the words and phrases in list B. Then write the phrases.

	A	B	
1	keep	a promise	1 *keep a secret*
2	break	a secret	2
3	take	no	3
4	feel	at someone	4
5	have	lies	5
6	laugh	nervous	6
7	say	it easy	7
8	tell	fun	8

6 Crossword

Complete the crossword and find this word ↓.

1 Try to pass an exam dishonestly.
2 To look at another student's work and write the same things.
3 Usual, not uncommon.
4 Something you don't tell other people.
5 Opposite of *tell the truth*.
6 Keep calm = Don't ...!
7 Stop worrying = ... it easy.
8 In a ... situation, everyone is treated equally.
9 A ... diet has a mixture of different types of food.
10 A friendly talk.
11 Sad, worried or angry.

7 Vocabulary

Complete the sentences with these verbs to make phrasal verbs with *down*.

calm   ~~lie~~   sit   slow   turn   write

1 If you don't feel well, you should *lie* down.
2 He was screaming and couldn't _____ down.
3 What's your address – can you _____ it down?
4 Come in and _____ down on the sofa.
5 _____ down! You're driving too fast.
6 Please _____ down the TV – it's too loud.

8 Pronunciation

Mark the stressed syllable.

■
concentrate   embarrassed   ignore

panic   promise   revision   upset

Extension Write a definition in your notebook for the ↓ word in exercise 6.

3 OPINIONS

4 Integrated Skills

Discussing facts and opinions

1 Reading

Read and complete with these words.

> borrowed   cost   die   dirty   fair   finish   much   pay   poorest   richer   school   sell   themselves   weapon

MAKE POVERTY HISTORY

FACTS

Half of the world's population lives on less than US$2 a day – that's about the (1) .... of a hamburger.

Every three seconds poverty takes someone's life – or to put it another way, about 30,000 people (2) .... every day as a result of poverty.

One woman dies every minute and a half while expecting or having a baby – and 99% of these women are in developing countries.

In the past, developing countries borrowed money from (3) .... countries. Now they have to pay for this. Every year the countries of Africa have to pay $15 billion to the richer countries. Some African countries spend more on paying this than on education.

In 2005, the UK stopped asking for money back from many of the world's (4) .... countries. What happens when countries don't have to pay for the money they (5) ....? In Tanzania, for example, children now don't have to (6) .... to go to primary school – as a result 66% more children go to school – and in Uganda 2.2 million people have clean water, which they didn't have before.

OPINIONS

'Education is the most powerful (7) .... which you can use to change the world,' said Nelson Mandela. We should make sure that every child in the world can go to (8) .... Education saves lives – children who (9) .... primary school are less than half as likely to get HIV/AIDS.

Aid needs to concentrate more on poor people's needs. We should spend more on health and education. Many people think that too (10) .... aid is spent on flights and hotels for 'experts' from the West.

We should listen to the poor people (11) ...., not only to their governments. Poor people expect aid to make their lives better, not to buy weapons and cars for the government.

Clean water is as much a human right as voting in a (12) .... election. But the richer countries are trying to make developing countries (13) .... their water companies – and the result is that people have to pay more for water. So people without enough money drink (14) .... water and get ill. We should make sure that everyone in the world has clean water.

You can make a difference – go to www.makepovertyhistory.org and find out more!

UNIT 3

2 Write a paragraph saying what you think about the facts and opinions in *Make Poverty History* on page 32.

I think that _____
We should _____
I agree/disagree that _____
I'm not saying _____
but _____
In my opinion, _____

3 Crossword

Complete the crossword.

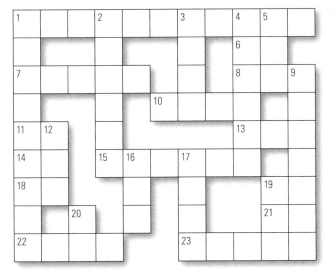

Across →
1 TVs, radios and computers need it. (11)
6 Opposite of *yes*. (2)
7 People get ... when things go wrong. (5)
8 The highest part of something. (3)
10 British children ... to stay at school until they're 16. (4)
11 They plan to break ... many laws ... possible. (2)
13 'I don't mind walking to school.' '... do I.' (3)
14 It's difficult ... know what to do. (2)
15 Opposite of *intelligent*. (6)
18 One ... three people can't read. (2)
19 We were hungry, ... we cooked some spaghetti. (2)
21 See 11 Across.
22 You shouldn't boil more water than you ... (4)
23 Buying and selling between countries. (5)

Down ↓
1 You go to school to get an ... (9)
2 My friend ... by copying my work in exams. (6)
3 Turning the TV off at the wall is a great ... (4)
4 Plan to do something. (6)
5 Also. (3)
9 Aim or goal. (7)
12 Opposite of *daughter*. (3)
16 We should ... to use less electricity. (3)
17 Someone who doesn't work all week works ...-time. (4)
19 Opposite of *happy*. (3)
20 Plural of *I*. (2)

LEARNER INDEPENDENCE

Talking to yourself: revising

You can talk in English on your own – by speaking, whispering or thinking in English. It's a great way of practising your English and of revising. As soon as you can after your English lesson, tell yourself as much as you can remember about it. Do the same again in the evening when you go to bed, and then again before your next English lesson.

Extensive reading

Read *The Treasure of Monte Cristo* and choose a short section which you like very much. First, read it to yourself several times silently in your head. Then read it again aloud, if possible recording your voice. Check the pronunciation of any words you are not sure of with a dictionary or your teacher. After that, work with a partner and practise reading to each other. Finally, read to a group of students or the whole class and say why you chose the section.

It is 1815. A ship returns to Marseilles, France, after a long voyage. On the ship is Edmond Dantès, who looks forward to seeing his beautiful girlfriend, Mercédès, again. Edmond and Mercédès plan to get married. But before they can marry, the new King's soldiers put Edmond in a terrible prison on an island. Why? Is it because of Edmond's meeting with Napoleon during the voyage? Will he escape and marry Mercédès?

3 OPINIONS
Inspiration EXTRA!

REVISION

LESSON 1

What are these things? Write sentences with *must* or *can't* using the words in brackets.

1 It has 36 passengers. (a car/a bus)
   It can't be a car. It must be a bus.

2 It's white and you drink it. (milk/tea)

3 You wear it when you ride a motorbike to protect you. (a cap/a helmet)

4 It's nearly twice as far from the Sun as Mercury. (Earth/Venus)

5 You use it to look at the stars. (a telescope/a mirror)

6 It tries to make you buy something. (an advertisement/a paperback)

7 It's more than a kilometre. (a mile/a metre)

8 It's a very popular pet. (a wolf/a dog)

LESSON 2

Use information from the chart you completed in exercise 2 on page 38 of the Student's Book to write sentences about the law in the UK using *must* or *can't*.

1 must/drive a car
   You must be 17 to drive a car.

2 can't/get married
   You can't get married until you're 16.

3 must/join the army

4 can't/vote in an election

5 must/live by yourself

6 can't/buy a pet

7 must/leave school

LESSON 3

Write sentences using *should* or *shouldn't*.

1 Some students at your school are bullying you.
   you/ignore them/show them that you are upset
   You should ignore them.
   You shouldn't show them that you are upset.

2 A friend misses the bus to school every day.
   he/stay in bed so long/get up earlier

3 Two students are shouting at each other.
   they/be more polite/be rude to each other

4 Your friend is very, very worried about an exam.
   she/calm down/panic

LESSON 4

Write questions for these answers about *Global Issues* on page 42 of the Student's Book.

1
   80%.

2
   A quarter of the world's population.

3
   Two and a half billion.

4
   24,000.

Spelling

Correct the spelling of these words from Unit 3 by doubling one letter in each word.

1 arest   2 buly   3 diference   4 forbiden   5 mod
6 ilegal   7 lotery   8 maried   9 miror   10 alowed

Brainteaser

What's the first thing you do in the morning?
Answer on page 49.

UNIT 3

EXTENSION

LESSON 1

Do you think there could be life on other planets? Write five sentences giving your opinion. Use *must* and *can't* at least once.

LESSON 2

Look at the chart you completed in exercise 2 on page 38 of the Student's Book and write five sentences about differences between the laws in the UK and your country.

LESSON 3

Read this message from *Teen Problem Page* and write some helpful advice.

I'm trying to do revision for my exams, but it's hard to concentrate for long. I sit on my bed with my books, but then I lie down and fall asleep. And my parents ask me to do things or my friends call for a chat or want me to go out with them, so I give up studying. The exam is next week and I'm starting to panic. What should I do?

LESSON 4

Look at the advice in *You Can Make A Difference!* on page 43 of the Student's Book. Then write a paragraph about how much (or how little) you are doing to save energy, and what you would like to do.

Web watch

Go to a charity website of your choice. Read more about aid and why it is needed. What did you find out? Make an *Aid* section in your vocabulary notebook.

Spelling

Read and complete the words from Unit 3.

The usual spelling of the sound /s/ is *s*, as in *arrest* or *against*. But in some words /s/ is written *c*, as in *cinema*.

1 di__tan__e   2 __ecret   3 con__entrate   4 differen__e
5 electri__ity   6 __en__ible   7 ni__ely   8 __urfa__e
9 __tupid   10 respon__ible   11 independen__e
12 purpo__e

Brainteaser

What word can't you say without breaking it?

Answer on page 49.

3 Culture

Good reads

Reading

Read the descriptions 1–3 of three novels and match them with the pictures A–C. Then match them with the extracts a–c.

1

Shake Hands For Ever
Ruth Rendell (born 1930)

This is one of 22 novels involving the character Detective Inspector Wexford, who lives and works in the fictional town of Kingsmarkham in south-eastern England. Wexford is a typical country policeman, and he is more interested in people, and the reasons for their crimes, than in clues or forensic evidence. In *Shake Hands For Ever*, Wexford has to spend some time in London looking for a man he believes is a murderer. But he is not really comfortable in large cities and he often gets lost.

2

Q&A: Slumdog Millionaire
Vikas Swarup (born 1963)

A boy from the slums of Mumbai answers all the questions on a TV quiz show correctly and wins a billion rupees. Everyone wants to know how a poor boy with little education could possibly know the answers. *Q&A: Slumdog Millionaire* tells the story of the main events in the boy's life which explain how he was able to answer the questions and win the contest.

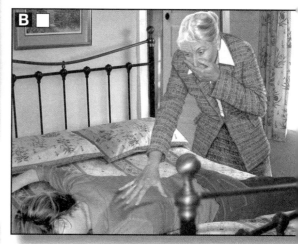

3

The Call of the Wild
Jack London (1876–1916)

Jack London was born in San Francisco in 1876. In the 1890s gold was found in the Yukon area of Canada. Jack London and many other people went there hoping to become rich. He never found any gold, but he became rich from his books and many of his stories are written about the Yukon. *The Call of the Wild* is about a dog called Buck. In winter the rivers freeze and people need dogs to help them carry things. Buck has several owners, but at the end of the story he lives with John Thornton, an American who is looking for gold. Thornton rescued Buck from a bad man who hit him and Buck loves Thornton very much.

a ☐

John Thornton had saved his life, but he was also the perfect master. His dogs were like children to him, and he never forgot a kind word for them. He loved to sit down with them for a long talk. But what Buck loved more than anything was when John Thornton put Buck's head between his hands with his own head on top and moved their heads from side to side. Sometimes, when Thornton did this, Buck felt so happy he thought his heart would fall out of his body. Then, when it was finished, he would jump to his feet, his mouth laughing.

And John Thornton would look at him and say, 'Well! You can almost speak.'

To show his love, Buck would take Thornton's hand in his mouth and press his teeth gently into it. But while Skeet and Nig were always waiting for Thornton to touch them, most of the time Buck was happy just to lie and watch him. Buck watched for hours, looking into Thornton's face for every thought, and following every move. Sometimes, John Thornton would feel Buck's eyes on him, and turn and look at him, his heart shining out of his eyes.

b ☐

Robert Hathall has brought his mother home to see his second wife, Angela. Mrs Hathall doesn't like Angela. She liked Robert's first wife, Eileen. She thinks the house will be dirty and untidy. Angela isn't at the station to meet them so Robert and his mother walk to the house.

After a minute or two, they came to Robert's cottage. Mrs Hathall was disappointed to see that it was a pleasant old house with brown bricks. Robert unlocked the front door.

'Angela, we're here!' he called.

Mrs Hathall followed him into the living room – and she was surprised. Where were the dirty tea-cups and the clothes across the chairs? Where was the dust on the furniture, the dirty windows? She had expected to see all of these things, but the place was amazingly clean.

'Where is Angela?' said Robert. 'I'm going out to the garage to look for the car. Go on upstairs, Mother. Your bedroom is the big room at the back.'

Mrs Hathall climbed the stairs, checking for dust. There was none. And her bedroom was as clean as the rest of the house. Disappointed, she went into the bathroom where there were clean towels and new soap. She washed her hands and came out again. The door to the main bedroom was half-open and Mrs Hathall looked inside.

A girl lay face-down on the bed. Mrs Hathall smiled coldly. Robert's wife was asleep. She was wearing shoes, old blue jeans and a red shirt. They were the same clothes that she had worn when they met at Earl's Court. Mrs Hathall remembered Eileen's pretty afternoon dresses. Eileen only slept in the afternoon when she was ill.

She walked across to the bed and looked down at the girl. She put a hand on the girl's shoulder to shake it. Then she stopped. The girl's neck was cold, and there was an ugly purple mark on it.

She was dead.

c ☐

The boys are at a carnival and they decide to visit a fortune-teller.

Salim paid his money and put out his hand. The fortune-teller looked at it. After a time, he said, 'I see a very good fortune for you.'

'Do you?' said Salim, pleased. 'What will I be?'

Mr Shastri closed his eyes for ten seconds, then opened them. 'You have a beautiful face,' he said. 'You will be a very famous actor.'

He turned to me. 'Do you want to show me your hand?'

'No, thank you,' I said, and I began to move away.

Salim stopped me. 'You have to show him your hand,' he said. 'Do it for me, please.'

So I gave the old man my ten rupees and held out my right hand. He looked at it for more than five minutes, then he made some notes.

'What's wrong?' asked Salim.

The fortune-teller shook his head. He did not look happy.

'You will have many problems,' he said. 'I can help you, but it will cost money.'

'How much?' I asked.

'Two hundred rupees,' he said. 'You could ask your father for the money. Is that his big bus?'

I laughed. 'We're not rich children,' I said. 'We're orphans from the Delhi Home for Boys. That bus doesn't belong to our father. You should have checked before telling us stories.'

Salim and I were walking away when the fortune-teller called to me. 'Listen,' he shouted. 'I want to give you something.'

I walked back and he gave me an old one-rupee coin. 'It's a lucky coin,' he said. 'Keep it. You will need it.'

Salim wanted an ice cream, but we had only one rupee and that would not buy us anything. Suddenly I dropped the coin. When I bent down to pick it up, I saw that it was lying next to a ten-rupee note which someone had dropped. So Salim and I bought ice creams and I put the coin carefully into my pocket. It *was* a lucky coin.

4 MIND OVER MATTER

1 She saw furniture moving

1 Reading

Read the story. Then read the sentences and write *T* (true) or *F* (false).

> One summer, Lucy went to stay with her aunt and uncle in an old house by the sea. She had a wonderful holiday – it was so different from life in the city. During the day, she went for long walks or sat on the warm sand and watched the boats floating on the waves and the birds flying over the beach. At night, she listened to her uncle telling stories about pirates and ghosts. One night she woke up and noticed the curtains in her room moving. Then she thought she heard someone singing outside. She got up and went over to the window. It was a dark night but the moon was shining brightly. Looking out over the garden, she thought she saw someone moving behind the big old tree next to the gate ...

1 Lucy and her parents didn't live by the sea. ☐
2 At night, Lucy listened to her aunt telling stories. ☐
3 She woke up one night because she heard singing. ☐
4 She saw her curtains moving. ☐
5 She couldn't see anything in the garden. ☐
6 She thought she saw her uncle going out of the gate. ☐

2 can/could + see

Look at the pictures and complete the sentences with phrases from the boxes.

| eat an ice cream   play football   ~~read a newspaper~~ |
| skateboard   sunbathe |

| phone a friend   say hello   sit on the ground   take a photo   wave |

1 I could see Anna *reading a newspaper*.
2 I could see Paul and Sue _____
3 I could see Bill _____
4 I could see Sam _____
5 I could see Jane _____

6 Now I can see Paul _____
7 Now I can see Sue _____
8 Now I can see Anna _____
9 Now I can see Jane _____
10 Now I can see Sam _____

3 Verbs of perception + present participle

Complete with the present participle of these verbs.

cook   describe   get   hold   play
~~ring~~   smile   sneeze   tell   touch

1 She heard the phone _ringing_ in the next room.
2 We watched the children _____ in the garden.
3 They listened to the farmer _____ his work.
4 She saw him _____ a bruise on his cheek.
5 I heard you _____ a lot earlier. Are you feeling better now?
6 He saw her _____ at him.
7 I noticed you _____ hands with your new friend.
8 Is lunch ready? I thought I smelt something nice _____.
9 I felt the water _____ cold and decided to leave the pool.
10 The investigator listened to Peggy _____ an incredible story.

4 can/could + feel, hear, see and smell

Complete with the present participle of these verbs.

burn   cheer   ~~come~~   blow   cry   get   melt   take off

1 He could hear the ambulance _coming_.
2 She could feel the wind _____ in her face.
3 We could smell the food _____.
4 They could hear the crowd _____.
5 I could see the ice _____.
6 You could feel the sea _____ rougher and rougher.
7 He could hear someone _____.
8 They could see the plane _____.

5 Vocabulary

The same letter is missing in each line. Write the complete words.

1 bruse   psychc   investgator
2 teror   recod   scaed
3 waling   knoc   quicly
4 hanted   broght   furnitre
5 flot   dughter   hirbrush
6 diffrent   strang   frightned

6 Crossword

Complete the crossword and find this word ↓.

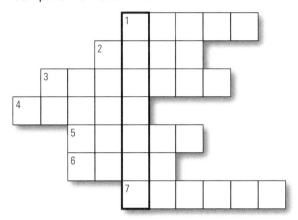

1 You do this when you hear something funny.
2 The sound of a bell.
3 Talk very quietly.
4 Speak in a very loud voice.
5 People do this when a footballer scores a goal.
6 A loud noise which fireworks make.
7 People do this when they are very frightened.

7 Pronunciation

Circle the two rhyming words in each line.

1 (float)   bought   (boat)
2 fright   light   hit
3 chair   cheer   hear
4 bruise   house   shoes
5 speak   week   break
6 dear   dare   wear
7 hold   cold   called
8 sneeze   size   knees

Extension Write an ending in your notebook for the story in exercise 1. Then compare your ending with another student's.

4 MIND OVER MATTER

2 I'll keep my fingers crossed!

1 Reading

Read the text and complete the sentences.

Ted has exams in a few weeks, but he hasn't done much work. His parents are worried about him. They know he is clever but they think he is lazy. They are afraid that he will fail his exams. They want him to go to university and get a good job. Ted wants to go to university, but not yet. First, he wants to play in a rock band and travel round the world. He thinks he will pass his exams easily and he doesn't understand why his parents are worried. Ted's teachers aren't worried about him, but they would like him to do a bit more work.

1 Ted's parents are worried that he _____ his exams.
2 Ted's teachers think he _____ his exams if he does a bit more work.
3 Ted's parents think he is clever but _____.
4 Ted isn't _____ about his exams.
5 Ted doesn't want to go to university _____.

2 will/won't

Write sentences using will/won't.

1 Ted's mother/afraid/leave home — *Ted's mother is afraid that he'll leave home.*
2 Ted's father/worried/pass his exams
3 Ted's brother and sister/think/be a famous rock star
4 Ted's best friend/sure/be all right
5 Ted's teachers/expect/go to university
6 Ted/know/pass his exams easily

3 shall and will/won't

Ted is revising for an exam. Write what different people offer and promise him using shall and will/won't.

1 Mother: do all I can to help
   I'll do all I can to help.

2 Father: not argue with you all the time

3 Brother: lend you my camera

4 Sister: cook you your favourite meal

5 Best friend: not ring you every five minutes

6 Uncle: test you on your work

7 Teacher: give you some practice tests

8 Neighbour: not play loud music

40

4 going to

Write sentences using *going to* and these phrases.

> break the law   dance all night   take a break
> not answer the phone   ~~play tennis~~

1 *She's going to play tennis.*

2 _____

3 _____

4 _____

5 _____

5 will and going to

Complete with *will* or *going to*.

WOMAN From the look on your face I can see that you (**1**) _____ be rude.

MAN I promise I (**2**) _____ (not) be.

WOMAN But I can see that you (**3**) _____ lose your temper.

MAN I hope that I (**4**) _____ (not), but I'm really angry.

WOMAN So we (**5**) _____ have an argument then. Please try to be polite.

MAN I (**6**) _____ do my best but it isn't easy.

WOMAN I don't want an argument. I've decided what I (**7**) _____ do. I (**8**) _____ go for a walk.

MAN OK. I think I (**9**) _____ come with you. I'd rather go for a walk than argue!

6 Vocabulary

Match the verbs in list A with the words and phrases in list B. Then write the phrases.

A	B	
1 cross	wood	1 *cross your fingers*
2 go	your fingers	2 _____
3 look	a horoscope	3 _____
4 keep	like	4 _____
5 read	to sleep	5 _____
6 touch	in touch	6 _____

7 Vocabulary

Complete the sentences with the correct form of these verbs to make phrasal verbs with *out*.

> ~~find~~   go   look   read   take   try

1 She's afraid that her friend will __*find*__ out what she said.
2 _____ out this new dictionary!
3 I can't _____ out – I have to study tomorrow.
4 He _____ two books out of the library.
5 _____ out! A car's coming.
6 Can you _____ out the menu? I don't have my glasses.

8 Vocabulary

Match the words with their definitions.

> accidentally   haunted   horoscope
> ladder   superstitious   take no notice

1 believing in the power of luck _____
2 it predicts your future from the stars _____
3 you climb up it _____
4 ignore _____
5 lived in by a ghost _____
6 by mistake _____

9 Pronunciation

Mark the stressed syllable.

■
acc**i**dentally   haunted   horoscope   ladder

notice   painter   supernatural   superstitious

> **Extension** Write three things that are lucky or unlucky in your country, but make one of them false. Can other students guess the false one?

4 MIND OVER MATTER
3 If you follow this advice ...

1 Reading

Read what the people are saying and complete using *'ll/won't* and these phrases.

> be an accident   get a big surprise   give you some   have enough money for the bus home
> pay for your driving lessons   ~~tell the teacher~~   win a lot of money

1

If you don't give me my calculator back, I *'ll tell the teacher*.

2

If you don't clean the car, I _____

3

If we buy any more, we _____

4

If I'm lucky, I _____

5

If you don't slow down, there _____

6

If you have a look here, you _____

7

If you ask nicely, I _____

2 First conditional

Match the beginnings and endings of these examples of Murphy's Law.

1 If you take an umbrella,   [f]
2 If you get to the bus stop early,   ☐
3 If you get to the bus stop late,   ☐
4 If you buy someone a new book as a present,   ☐
5 If you wash the car,   ☐
6 If you sit in the sun,   ☐
7 If you look for something at the back of a book,   ☐
8 If you can't find something you're looking for,   ☐

a it'll get cloudy.
b it'll rain.
c it'll be in the last place you look.
d you'll find it at the front.
e the bus will be early.
f ~~it won't rain.~~
g someone else will give them the same one.
h the bus will be late.

42

3 First conditional

Write questions and answers.

1 what/you/do/it/rain?
   What will you do if it rains?
   we/have the picnic indoors
   We'll have the picnic indoors.

2 what/you/say/she/ask what happened?
   I/tell the truth

3 how/you/get home/school/finish early?
   Anna/give me a lift

4 who/you/tell/you/pass your driving test?
   I/tell everyone

5 what/you/buy/parents/give you some money?
   I/get a new pair of shoes

6 who/you/ask/you/need help?
   I/ask my brother

4 Vocabulary

Find eight words in the word square from the *Memory Power* article on page 52 of the Student's Book.

C	O	N	N	E	C	T	I	O	N	S
E	A	W	Y	V	A	P	B	E	E	M
R	C	L	W	E	F	O	R	G	E	T
E	K	I	I	S	S	E	E	F	S	I
C	N	N	C	T	T	A	M	O	W	N
A	O	K	A	R	E	P	E	A	T	E
L	P	L	E	A	N	L	M	R	I	R
L	M	E	M	O	R	A	B	L	E	S
X	B	A	U	L	Y	P	E	R	L	S
C	O	N	C	E	N	T	R	A	T	E

Use the words from the word square to complete these sentences.

1 You won't *remember* new information if you don't get enough sleep.

2 _____ names, numbers and directions as soon as you hear them.

3 You won't _____ things you have to do if you write them down in a diary.

4 People can often _____ lists of different things if they make _____ between them.

5 It's easier to learn new information if you _____ it to something you already know.

6 Personalised information is often more _____.

7 Most people study in a quiet place because it is easier to _____.

5 Pronunciation

Complete the chart with these words.

attention calendar concentrate connection direction easier memorable memory organise remember similar together

■ ▪ ▪	▪ ■ ▪
	attention

Extension Answer these questions for yourself in your notebook.

What will you do if ...?

1 you have too much homework tonight
2 the weather is good at the weekend
3 a friend invites you to supper tonight
4 you wake up very early tomorrow morning
5 you take the wrong bag home from school tomorrow
6 the school is closed when you get there tomorrow morning

4 MIND OVER MATTER

Integrated Skills
Telling a story

1 Reading

Read sections A–G from a detective story called *The Woman Who Disappeared* and complete them with these phrases.

a   with his arm in the air
b   it was a knife
c   as the men ran into the door
d   and tried to pull away from me
e   in the middle of the dance floor
f   as hard as I could
g   and they dropped their knives
h   and they both followed me

Lenny Samuel is a private detective in Los Angeles. It's midnight and he's in a nightclub. Two men, called Jo and Ginger, want to talk to Lenny about a dead man. But Lenny doesn't want to talk to them. Lenny sees Jo in the nightclub and starts to leave. But when he opens the front door, Ginger is waiting outside.

THE FIGHT

A
I stopped and looked behind me. Jo was closer now and the smile on his face looked very unfriendly. I was caught. I couldn't go out of the door because Ginger was there, and Jo was right behind me.
   I turned around and ran quickly towards Jo. Before he knew what I was doing, I put my arms around him and started dancing. Jo was very surprised (**1**) _____.
But he couldn't fight properly. He was afraid that the other people in the club would notice.
   I looked over my shoulder and saw Ginger moving towards us. I pushed Jo into a crowd of dancers (**2**) _____.

B
The door was locked but I kicked it open. As I ran out into the dark street, I could still hear people shouting in the nightclub. I ran to my car and opened the door. Just then there was a noise behind me. I turned around and saw a man (**3**) _____. Then I felt a terrible pain in my head. Everything went black and I fell to the ground, unconscious.

C
Jo gave a cry of pain and fell to the floor. I looked around. Ginger was pushing his way through the dancers towards me. I turned and ran off the dance floor. Ginger helped Jo up (**4**) _____. I ran between the tables where people were eating. I looked back, slipped and fell over. As I fell, I knocked a table and the plates of food and glasses fell on top of me.

D
There was a loud bang as the gun went off. The bang was followed by a scream of pain from one of the cooks, who fell down holding his foot.
   I quickly picked up a large pile of dirty plates and threw them at Jo and Ginger. Jo saw the plates coming and tried to move away. But he slipped on the wet floor and Ginger fell on top of him. Without waiting, I ran to a door at the back of the kitchen.

E
I pushed the food off, got to my feet, and saw a door marked 'Kitchen'. I ran through the door into the kitchen. Then I stopped and held the door open. As Jo and Ginger reached the door I closed it in their faces. There was a loud bang (**5**) _____.
   I smiled and turned around. But I didn't smile for very long. Three cooks were coming towards me with big kitchen knives in their hands.

F
Then I felt something sharp touching my back. (**6**) _____.
   'Stop trying to be funny, Samuel,' Jo said angrily. 'Stop dancing now and go over to the door.'
   Ginger was still quite a long way away from us. I saw some of the other people stopping dancing. They were looking in surprise at two men dancing together with one of them holding a knife! I lifted my foot and kicked Jo's leg (**7**) _____.

G
I looked at the cooks and their knives. I thought about fighting them. I decided it was a stupid idea to try to fight three big men with knives.
   Then I saw a big saucepan of soup on the stove. I picked the saucepan up and threw it at the cooks. There were cries of pain as the hot soup hit the cooks (**8**) _____.
   Just then, the door opened behind me. Jo and Ginger stood in the doorway and Ginger was holding a gun.

44

2 Now read *The Fight* again and put the sections in the right order. Section A is the first section.

3 Complete these sentences using information from the story on page 44.

1 When Lenny and Jo were dancing, Jo _____

2 Some of the other dancers were surprised when they saw _____

3 Lenny closed the kitchen door _____

4 When Lenny turned around in the kitchen, he saw _____

5 Lenny threw the soup _____

6 Ginger shot _____ by mistake.

7 When Lenny threw the plates, _____

8 When Lenny got to his car, _____

4 Crossword

Complete the crossword.

Across →

1 People who have really good ... don't forget the things they've learnt. (8)
6 It helps to ... connections between things in a list. (4)
7 Another word for *remember*. (6)
9 Say something again. (6)
11 Sunday is the last day of the ... (4)
12 A dark mark on the skin. (6)
14 I'm not good at remembering names ... numbers. (2)
15 Many people find it ... to study in a quiet place. (6)
16 Some people think houses are haunted by the ghosts of ... people. (4)

Down ↓

1 If information is personalised, it becomes more ... (9)
2 The first number. (3)
3 You see with these. (4)
4 Some people think breaking a mirror is ... (7)
5 Superstitious people won't walk under this. (6)
8 The fourth planet from the Sun. (4)
10 When it rains hard, we say it ... (5)
11 You can look this up in a dictionary. (4)
13 You hear with this. (3)

LEARNER INDEPENDENCE

Listening skills

Match the questions (1–5) with the techniques for being a good listener (a–e).

1 'I'm sorry, what does "slip" mean?' ☐
2 'Excuse me, could you say that last bit again?' ☐
3 'Do you mean that one of the men hit him?' ☐
4 'Did you say "saucepan"?' ☐
5 'The detective threw the ... – what?' ☐

a Repeat up to the part you didn't understand, then ask for help.
b Repeat a word to check if you heard correctly.
c Ask the speaker to repeat what they said.
d Say what you think the speaker meant.
e Ask the speaker to explain a word.

Extensive reading

Read *The Great Gatsby*. Then write short descriptions of Jay Gatsby, Tom Buchanan, Jordan Baker and Daisy Buchanan, but use A, B, C and D or *he/she* instead of their names. Give your descriptions to another student and ask him/her to identify the characters.

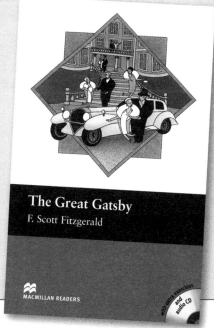

F. Scott Fitzgerald's famous love story is set in New York in 1922. Nick Carraway has a house on Long Island next door to Jay Gatsby, who is rich and handsome. No one knows where Gatsby or his money came from. Everyone in New York goes to Gatsby's fantastic parties. But Gatsby is interested in only one person, Daisy Buchanan. Daisy is Nick's cousin and she is young, beautiful and unhappily married.

4 MIND OVER MATTER

Inspiration EXTRA!

REVISION

LESSON 1

Imagine you were at these places yesterday. Write sentences using *could* and the verb in brackets.

1 The railway station
   I could see a train leaving. (see)
2 A football match
   _____ (hear)
3 The park
   _____ (see)
4 A beach
   _____ (feel)
5 The kitchen at home
   _____ (smell)
6 The town centre
   _____ (hear)

LESSON 2

Complete using *will/won't* and these phrases.

> finish in time   happen again today   have a party
> like it   ~~rain~~   be angry   see her again   forget

1 We're going to have a picnic tomorrow so I hope it
   won't rain.
2 On my next birthday I hope I _____
3 I've got a present for my best friend – I hope he _____
4 It's only ten minutes to the end of the exam. I hope I _____
5 She's great fun – I hope I _____
6 I missed the bus yesterday – I hope it _____
7 He promised to call so I hope he _____
8 I'm late again. I hope my parents _____

LESSON 3

Match the beginnings with the endings.

STUDYING FOR EXAMS

1 Don't study too late at night. If you don't get enough sleep, ☐
2 Listen carefully and read thoughtfully. If you concentrate, ☐
3 Make a revision timetable. If you plan your revision, ☐
4 Make lists. If you make lists, ☐
5 Try to personalise information. If you personalise it, ☐
6 Repeat things. If you repeat things as you learn them, ☐

a it will be more memorable.
b you won't run out of time before the exam.
c you won't forget things.
d you'll find it easier to remember new things.
e your brain won't be able to process new information.
f they will stay in your memory longer.

LESSON 4

Match these words with their definitions.

1 adore   a angry
2 confess   b say that you did something wrong
3 in charge of   c wear
4 get over   d artificial hair
5 honeymoon   e love someone very much
6 put on   f holiday after a marriage
7 cross   g recover from
8 wig   h be reponsible for

Spelling

Fill in the missing letter in each of these words.

1 a__cidentally 2 confes__ 3 conclu__ion 4 for__cast
5 honeymo__n 6 hor__scope 7 impat__ently 8 lad__er
9 not__ce 10 perso__alise 11 reca__l 12 supernat__ral
13 superstiti__us 14 ter__or 15 verdi__t 16 wor__ied

Brainteaser

The more there is of it, the less you see.
Answer on page 49.

UNIT 4

EXTENSION

LESSON 1

Imagine that you witnessed a robbery. Write sentences beginning *I saw/heard someone/something ...*

1 *I heard a police car driving fast.*
2
3
4
5
6
7
8

LESSON 2

Write three sentences using *hope + will/won't*. Then write three sentences predicting the future from present evidence using *going to*.

1 *I hope that lunch will be ready soon.*
2
3
4
5 *It's 12 o'clock already! I'm going to be late.*
6
7
8

LESSON 3

Complete the sentences for yourself about tomorrow.

1 If I finish my homework early, *I'll go for a swim.*
2 If my parents agree,
3 If I go to bed late,
4 If a friend asks me to go to the cinema,
5 If I fall over and hurt myself,
6 If I have enough time,
7 If I don't have enough time,
8 If I'm lucky,

LESSON 4

Write a short review of *Rebecca*.

Web Watch

Search for 'Superstitions' on the Internet and find four funny or strange superstitions. Look up new words in the dictionary and make a *Superstitions* section in your vocabulary notebook.

Spelling

Read and complete the words with *g* or *j*.

When we hear the sound /dʒ/ before the letters *i*, *e* or *y*, the usual spelling is *g*, as in **age**. When we hear the sound /dʒ/ before the letters *a*, *o* or *u*, the usual spelling is *j*, as in **job**.

1 chan___e 2 ___oke 3 cotta___e 4 ori___inal 5 ___une
6 ___acket 7 ___anuary 8 ___eans 9 ___ob 10 char___e
11 ___ourney 12 ___ym 13 ___uly 14 ___ust

Brainteaser

Make one word from the letters in *new door*.

Answer on page 49.

REVIEW
UNITS 3–4

1 Read about life in outer space. Then read the sentences and choose *True*, *False* or *Doesn't say*.

IS THERE LIFE IN OUTER SPACE?

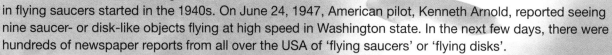

A recent survey showed that 61% of British teenagers believe in aliens and UFOs. And 40% of people in the USA believe that intelligent aliens have visited Earth.

The idea that aliens might visit Earth in flying saucers started in the 1940s. On June 24, 1947, American pilot, Kenneth Arnold, reported seeing nine saucer- or disk-like objects flying at high speed in Washington state. In the next few days, there were hundreds of newspaper reports from all over the USA of 'flying saucers' or 'flying disks'.

The following month, there was the most famous event in the history of aliens and UFOs. In July 1947, William Brazel discovered a strange object on his ranch in the desert about 75 miles from the small town of Roswell in New Mexico. Brazel informed the local sheriff, and an army report described the object as a flying saucer. Later the army changed the story and said the object was only a weather balloon. But people who lived near Brazel's ranch saw a strange blue light shining over the desert in the middle of the night. Later, there were other reports from locals who saw people carrying bodies of dead aliens to Roswell Air Force base. Many people believed the US government was trying to hide the true story: aliens were visiting Earth. And of course, if aliens really landed near Roswell, the US government might not want people to know!

Could there be life out there? Some scientists believe that there may be thousands of planets with intelligent creatures. That's why Voyager 1 and Voyager 2 carried recordings into space with information about life on Earth: photographs of people, animals and plants, greetings in 54 languages, the song of a whale, and music from all over the world. If aliens exist, and if they find the recordings, will they contact Earth? And will they be friendly?

1 Nearly two-thirds of British teenagers believe in aliens and UFOs.
   A True   **B** False   **C** Doesn't say

2 60% of Americans don't believe in aliens and UFOs.
   A True   **B** False   **C** Doesn't say

3 Kenneth Arnold was flying when he saw nine flying saucers.
   A True   **B** False   **C** Doesn't say

4 William Brazel told a sheriff about the strange object on his ranch.
   A True   **B** False   **C** Doesn't say

5 The first army report said the object was a weather balloon.
   A True   **B** False   **C** Doesn't say

6 People in Roswell saw a blue light shining over the desert.
   A True   **B** False   **C** Doesn't say

7 There were lots of newspaper reports about dead aliens at Roswell.
   A True   **B** False   **C** Doesn't say

8 Voyager 1 and Voyager 2 carried information about our planet.
   A True   **B** False   **C** Doesn't say

2 Complete with the correct form of the words in capitals.

1 It is _____ to eat a balanced diet. SENSE
2 I'm not _____, but I often read my horoscope. SUPERSTITION
3 It's a romantic novel, and the ending is very _____. DRAMA
4 If you do enough _____, you'll pass the exam. REVISE
5 Sara is so _____. She makes everyone feel better. CHEER
6 I don't care – it makes no _____ to me. DIFFERENT
7 500 million people in Africa have no _____. ELECTRIC
8 We saw a _____ film about the universe. MEMORY

3 Complete the second sentence so that it means the same as the first sentence.

1 I'm sure your watch is wrong.
   Your watch must _____
2 It is impossible that this animal is a crocodile.
   This animal _____
3 It isn't necessary to book tickets for the film.
   You don't have _____
4 It's illegal for children in the UK to buy lottery tickets.
   Children in the UK can't _____
5 Turn down the music and it will be easier to concentrate.
   If _____
6 I can do the washing up for you.
   Shall I _____
7 You ought to phone to say you'll be late.
   You'd better _____
8 I promise to email you every day.
   I'll _____

4 Find the odd word.

1 (orbit) moon planet star
2 cycle drive fly promise
3 bully doctor reporter detective
4 confident nervous worried upset
5 electricity energy gas oil
6 look play sound taste
7 forget recall remember remind

Answers to Brainteasers

UNIT 3
Revision wake up
Extension silence

UNIT 4
Revision darkness or fog
Extension one word

LEARNER INDEPENDENCE
SELF ASSESSMENT

Vocabulary

1 Draw this chart in your notebook. How many words can you write in each category?

More than 10? Good!   *More than 12?* Very good!
More than 15? Excellent!

Space	
Sounds	
Books	

2 Put the words in order to make expressions from the phrasebooks in Lesson 4 in Units 3 and 4.

1 other in words
   In other words ...
2 what I do should
3 getting up fed it with I'm
4 it more any take can't I
5 difference makes no it
6 crossed I'll fingers my keep
7 safe a have journey
8 only you're the one not

Check your answers.
8/8 Excellent!   6/8 Very good!   4/8 Try again!

My learning diary
In Units 3 and 4:
My favourite topic is _____
My favourite picture is _____
The three lessons I like most are _____
My favourite activity or exercise is _____
Something I don't understand is _____
Something I want to learn more about is _____

5 CHALLENGES

1 Has she learnt first aid yet?

1 Reading

Read the article and complete it with the verbs in the present perfect.

'IF I CAN DO IT AT 13, THEN ANYBODY CAN,' SAYS YOUNGEST EVEREST CLIMBER

At the age of 13, Jordan Romero (1) _____ (become) the youngest person to climb Mount Everest. More than 4,000 people (2) _____ (reach) the top of the world's highest mountain since Edmund Hillary and Tenzing Norgay Sherpa first climbed it in 1953, but even more people (3) _____ (give up) because the climb is just too challenging for them.

Jordan (4) _____ (replace) 16-year-old Temba Tsheri Sherpa as the youngest person to reach the top. Other mountains he (5) _____ (climb) include Mount Kilimanjaro in Africa and Mount Aconcagua in South America.

Mountain climbing (6) _____ (be) a favourite hobby of the Romero family for some time. They spent over a year preparing for the trip and Jordan's father accompanied him on his successful climb. They all said that standing at the top of Everest was a feeling like no other.

Jordan (7) _____ now _____ (return) to his home in California and he (8) _____ (go back) to school. But he (9) _____ already _____ (start) to plan his next challenge – he will spend the summer climbing the highest mountains in all 50 American states.

2 Present perfect with *just*

Write sentences about what has just happened using *just* and these phrases.

> break a window   get married   ~~have an accident~~
> miss the train   score a goal   win a prize

1 *They've just had an accident.*

2 _____

3 _____

4 _____

5 _____

6 _____

3 Present perfect with *already* and *yet*

Jackie is having a birthday party at home this evening. Look at the list and write sentences saying what she has already done, and what she hasn't done yet.

1 *She's already invited all her friends.*
2
3
4
5
6
7
8

4 Present perfect with *already* and *yet*

Students Julie and Simon are going to South America tomorrow for a backpacking holiday. Write questions using the present perfect, and answers with *already* or *yet*.

1 choose clothes to take ✗
JULIE *Have you chosen clothes to take?*
SIMON *No, I haven't chosen them yet.*
2 buy some walking boots ✓
JULIE
SIMON
3 change some money ✗
JULIE
SIMON
4 book a taxi to the airport ✓
JULIE
SIMON
5 look at the map ✓
JULIE
SIMON
6 find your passport ✗
JULIE
SIMON

5 Vocabulary

Compare the words in list A with the words in list B. Write *S* if they have almost the same meaning, *O* if they are opposites, and *G* if A is more general than B.

	A	B	
1	pair	couple	S
2	performer	actor	
3	journey	trip	
4	arrive	leave	
5	travel	ride	
6	world	Earth	
7	challenging	easy	
8	complete	finish	

6 Vocabulary

Match these words and phrases with *GO* or *HAVE*.

> ~~an accident~~ camping fun home on holiday
> an idea a look a meal a party a picnic red
> skiing to sleep wrong

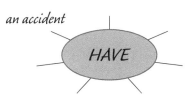

7 Pronunciation

Write these words under *Star* or *Wars*.

> ~~army~~ board calm charm heart law party
> quarter start toward war warm

/ɑː/ **star**	/ɔː/ **wars**
army	

> **Extension** Make a list of all the things you have to do this week. Which ones have you already done and which ones haven't you done yet? Write sentences in your notebook.

5 CHALLENGES

2 Have you ever wondered …?

1 Reading

Read the story and answer the questions.

Yesterday, Sherlock Holmes and Dr Watson went camping and they put up their tent in a field. It is now the middle of the night, and Holmes wakes Watson up.

'What's the matter?' Watson asks. 'Why on earth have you woken me up?'

'Look up', Holmes says. 'What can you see?'

Watson looks up at the sky. 'I can see millions and millions of stars.'

Holmes smiles. 'And what does that tell you?' he asks.

'It tells me that tomorrow is going to be a beautiful day – I have never seen so many stars! What does it tell you, Holmes?'

'It tells me that someone has stolen our tent!'

1 When did Holmes and Watson go camping?

2 Where did they put up their tent?

3 Why has Holmes woken Watson up?

4 Why does Watson say that tomorrow is going to be a beautiful day?

5 Why can they see the stars?

2 Present perfect with *ever* and *never*

Complete with the verbs in the present perfect and *ever* or *never*.

EMMA (**1**) *Have* you *ever wondered* (wonder) what it's like on Mars?

JAKE It's a long way from Earth, isn't it? That's why no one (**2**) _____ (go) there.

EMMA What about the Moon? (**3**) _____ you _____ (imagine) landing on the Moon?

JAKE Yes, but I (**4**) _____ (want) to go there.

EMMA (**5**) _____ you _____ (think) about space tourism?

JAKE You mean holidays in space? I (**6**) _____ (hear) anything so crazy!

EMMA So you (**7**) _____ (feel) excited about space travel, have you?

JAKE Yes, I have, but it's not for me. I (**8**) _____ (enjoy) flying!

UNIT 5

3 Present perfect with *ever* and past simple

Write questions and answers.

1. Sophie/go to Spain/half term
   Has Sophie ever been to Spain?
   Yes, she has. She went to Spain at half term.
2. Stella/win a prize/last month
3. Darren/fly a plane/two years ago
4. Nick and Lorna/perform their songs on TV/last night
5. Anna/play football/a week ago
6. Emily and Alex/try salsa dancing/last weekend

4 Present perfect with *ever/never* and past simple

Write questions and answer them for yourself.

1. fly a kite
   Have you ever flown a kite?
   No, I've never flown a kite.   OR   *Yes, I have. I flew a kite last summer.*
2. roll down a hill
3. climb a mountain
4. do a parachute jump
5. drive a car
6. swim in a river or a lake
7. ride a horse

5 Vocabulary

Complete the sentences with these verbs.

> contain   float   imagine   involves
> roll   speed   steer   wonder

1. It's quite easy to _____ in salt water.
2. Can you _____ being on a giant rollercoaster?
3. I _____ what paragliding feels like.
4. Free running _____ climbing and jumping.
5. It's fun to _____ down a hill in a zorbing sphere.
6. How much water does this bottle _____?
7. I'll give directions and you _____ the boat.
8. You _____ through the water on water-skis.

6 Vocabulary

Match the words in list A with the words in list B and write six compound nouns.

	A	B		
1	beach	skiing	1	*beach ball*
2	bungee	hockey	2	
3	ice	surfing	3	
4	kite	jumping	4	
5	motor	ball	5	
6	water	bike	6	

7 Pronunciation

Complete the chart with these words according to the pronunciation of *ch*.

> ~~beach~~   challenge   champagne   change
> character   cheer   Czech   machine
> parachute   psychic   technique

/k/	/tʃ/	/ʃ/
	beach	

> **Extension** Write sentences in your notebook about three amazing things people you know have done and make one false. Show your sentences to another student and see if they can guess the false one.

5 CHALLENGES
3 We've been friends ever since we met

1 Reading

Read and complete the text with these words.

achieved   been   broken   crossed   done   felt   for (x3)   landed   loved   said   saved   sent   since (x3)   slept   suffered   told

MACARTHUR BREAKS ROUND-THE-WORLD RECORD

People all over the globe have (1) _____ congratulations to sailor Ellen MacArthur (2) _____ she broke the non-stop round-the-world record last night. MacArthur (3) _____ a 'finish line' in the sea between France and England late on 7 February after sailing solo round the world (4) _____ 71 days, 14 hours, 18 minutes and 33 seconds. The 28-year-old has (5) _____ Frenchman Francis Joyon's 2004 world record of 72 days and 23 hours.

After she (6) _____ the record time, MacArthur (7) _____ : 'I'm absolutely over the moon but I feel exhausted. When I crossed the line, I (8) _____ like falling asleep.'

(9) _____ 28 November 2004, when she began the 27,000 mile voyage, MacArthur has (10) _____ an average of 30 minutes at a time (11) _____ a total of four hours a day.

'It's (12) _____ an extraordinary experience, quite overwhelming,' MacArthur (13) _____ a crowd of 8,000 people when she finally (14) _____ on the south coast of England. 'I have never in my life (15) _____ anything so difficult. I don't think I'll ever manage to communicate how difficult this has been.'

Fortunately, MacArthur has never (16) _____ from sea-sickness. She has (17) _____ being at sea (18) _____ she was a child – she (19) _____ her pocket money and school lunch money (20) _____ three years to buy her first boat at the age of ten!

2 Reading

Read the sentences and write *T* (true) or *F* (false). Correct the false sentences.

1 Ellen made some stops during her trip around the world. ☐

2 She sailed on her own. ☐

3 She wasn't happy when she broke Joyon's record. ☐

4 She slept exactly 30 minutes at a time. ☐

5 It was easy for Ellen to explain how hard the trip was. ☐

6 Sailing doesn't make Ellen feel sick. ☐

54

UNIT 5

3 for and since

Complete the phrases with *for* or *since*.

1 _____ 1999
2 _____ a few days
3 _____ a fortnight
4 _____ 1st September
5 _____ last winter
6 _____ a long time
7 _____ a moment
8 _____ half past two
9 _____ she came home
10 _____ five years
11 _____ last week
12 _____ ten seconds
13 _____ midnight
14 _____ two months
15 _____ we first met
16 _____ yesterday morning

4 Present perfect with *for* and *since*

Write questions beginning *How long ...?* and answer them using *for* or *since*.

1 Nicki/know/Tom – two years
   How long has Nicki known Tom?
   She's known him for two years.

2 Lorna and Nick/be at *Star School* – last month

3 Dan Deacon/play in a rock band – he left school

4 you/have your new mobile – ten days

5 Sophie/live in Liverpool – she was 12

6 she/want to be a doctor – a very long time

7 they/be married – six years

5 The preposition *for*

We use the preposition *for* to say how long something lasted, but we use it in other ways too. In these sentences, *for* is missing. Write *for* in the correct position.

1 The student apologised to the teacher **for** being late.
2 Why don't we go a swim in the sea?
3 Did you get lots of presents your birthday?
4 I went abroad the first time when I was 13.
5 Usain Bolt is famous winning Olympic® gold medals.
6 I'd like you to do this exercise homework.
7 How much did you have to pay your camera?
8 It's difficult me to concentrate on my work.
9 Are you still waiting the phone to ring?
10 I've looked everywhere my glasses, but I can't find them.

6 Vocabulary

Match the words in list A with the words in list B and write six compound nouns.

	A	B		
1	world	book	1	*world record*
2	course	school	2	
3	drug	medal	3	
4	gold	record	4	
5	personal	test	5	
6	high	assistant	6	

7 Pronunciation

Circle the two rhyming words in each line.

1	phone	(done)	(won)
2	sorry	worry	lorry
3	gold	hold	could
4	head	speed	said
5	case	phrase	race
6	start	heart	hurt
7	house	course	horse
8	year	wear	steer
9	down	known	town

Extension Write a short paragraph about a famous sports person that you admire.

5.4 CHALLENGES

Integrated Skills
Describing personal experiences

1 Reading

Sophie is on a school trip in France. Read and complete her email with these words.

> after   ago   already   always   because   but   ever   for   just   never   next   since   so   yet

From: Sophie
To: Mum
Subject: The best trip ever!

This is the best holiday I've (1) _____ had! We're spending a week in Morzine, a ski resort in the French Alps. It's summer of course, (2) _____ we can't go skiing or snowboarding, but there are loads of exciting things to do, like windsurfing and mountain biking.

We've been really busy (3) _____ we arrived here three days (4) _____. We've (5) _____ tried windsurfing on Lake Geneva – that was on the first day. But I wasn't very good at it – I got very wet (6) _____ I kept falling off the board! And today, guess what – I've (7) _____ been paragliding! I was strapped to a paragliding pilot, and we ran down a steep grass mountain slope. Suddenly we took off – whoosh – and we floated in the sky over the mountains (8) _____ about 25 minutes. It's something I've (9) _____ wanted to do and it was magic!

Tomorrow we're going to climb up a mountain and spend the night camping under the stars. We're going to make a campfire and cook our own food. And the (10) _____ day we're going to whizz down the mountain on mountain bikes.

We're staying in a really nice hotel, and we've had great food – we've all been very hungry (11) _____ exhausting days out. There's a swimming pool next to the hotel, (12) _____ I haven't had a chance to go for a swim (13) _____. I've (14) _____ had so much fun in all my life!

2

Rob's parents have won a holiday in Egypt. It's now the evening on Day 5. Look at the itinerary and write their email to Rob. Include this information.

- Where are they now?
- How did they get there?
- Where have they already been?
- What have they done?
- Where are they going next?
- What haven't they done yet?

We've just arrived in _____

ITINERARY

Day 1 Fly to Cairo, Egypt.
Day 2 See the Pyramids and the Sphinx. Sail in a boat on the Nile.
Day 3 Visit the Egyptian Museum. Go shopping in the bazaars.
Day 4 Ride camels in the desert.
Day 5 Travel by train to Alexandria. Go sightseeing.
Days 6&7 Return to Cairo and fly to Luxor. Visit the temples of Luxor and Karnak.
Day 8 Visit the Valley of the Kings and Queens.
Day 9 Fly to the Red Sea.
Day 10 Go scuba diving.
Day 11 Fly home.

56

3 Crossword

Complete the crossword.

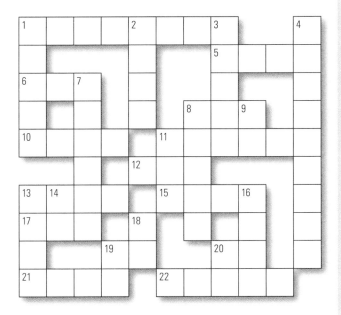

Across →

1. Have you ever ... what it's like inside a washing machine? (8)
5. Opposite of *poor*. (4)
6. A kind of music. (3)
8. See 17 Across.
10. The lake is very ... – you can't see the bottom. (4)
11. Opposite of *went down*. (4, 2)
12. Something you can keep things in ... (3)
13. The film has ... started – you haven't missed anything. (4)
15. The opposite of *put down* is ... up. (4)
17, 8 You ... a ... to plan the route of a journey. (3, 3)
19. Would you like to go ... a boat trip? (2)
20. The motorbike was travelling ... 100km an hour. (2)
21. Opposite of *pull*. (4)
22. The Inca trail ... to over 4,000 metres. (5)

Down ↓

1. Lake Titicaca is one of the highest lakes in the ... (5)
2. Have you ... tried snowboarding? (4)
3. I have always wanted to win a gold medal and now my ... has come true. (5)
4. Olympic gold medal winners are the ... in their sport. (9)
7. A word you use to ask for something politely. (6)
8. Something wonderful, with mystery. (5)
9. Short for *physical education*. (2)
11. A kind of hat. (3)
13. It must be exciting to do a parachute ... (4)
14. *let's = let* ... (2)
16. You stand on a small surfboard when you are ...-surfing. (4)
18. I didn't get up ... time to have breakfast. (2)
19. People say '...!' when they are surprised. (2)
20. There are wild animals such ... llamas in Peru. (2)

UNIT 5

LEARNER INDEPENDENCE

Vocabulary skills

Read the questions about techniques for developing vocabulary and assess your skills using the scale below.

How good are you at ...

- guessing the meaning of new words in a text?
- recognising compound words?
- recognising prefixes and suffixes?
- keeping your vocabulary notebook up to date?
- writing definitions of words?
- making word maps?

5 = Very good.
4 = Good.
3 = OK.
2 = Not sure.
1 = Not very good.

Now compare with another student. Work together and make a word map – like the one on page 9 – to help you learn words from Unit 5.

Extensive reading

Look at the picture on the front cover of *The Eye of the Tiger*. What do you think 'the eye of the tiger' is? And where do you think it is found? Then read the book and see if you are right.

Now look at the picture on page 5 of the book. Who are the five men? Write about what happens to each of them in the end.

Harry Fletcher has left a life of international crime behind him, and now organises fishing trips in his boat from an island off the East African coast. But when he meets some very dangerous men who know about his past, he has to use all his talents to survive.

5 CHALLENGES

Inspiration EXTRA!

REVISION

LESSON 1

Answer the questions using the present perfect with *already* or *yet*.

1 Does Sophie want to see the film *Rio*?
   No – *she's already seen it.*
2 Do Julie and Simon want to go to Brazil?
   Yes – *they haven't been there yet.*
3 Does Nick want to sing his song on TV?
   Yes –
4 Does Rob want to read *The Sign of Four*?
   No –
5 Do Jack and Emma want to have lunch?
   No –
6 Does Ted want to download the new Adele album?
   Yes –

LESSON 2

Write questions and short answers.

1 Steve/try bungee-jumping? ✗
   Has Steve ever tried bungee jumping?
   No, he hasn't.
2 Lisa/go sailing ✓

3 Joni and Sara/play ice hockey? ✗

4 Lorna/do aerobics? ✓

5 Rob/win a race? ✗

6 Ted/ride a motorbike? ✓

7 Julie/ski down a mountain? ✗

LESSON 3

Write questions using the present perfect. Then answer them for yourself.

1 how long/you/be/in the same class?
   How long have you been in the same class?
   Since
2 how long/you/have/English lessons?

   For
3 how long/you/have/the same English teacher?

   Since
4 how long/you/know/your best friend?

   For
5 how long/you/sleep/in the same room at home?

   Since

LESSON 4

Match expressions 1–5 with their meanings. Choose from a–h.

1 It didn't really matter. ☐
2 It was well worth it. ☐
3 I didn't have a clue. ☐
4 I couldn't face it. ☐
5 It was magic. ☐

a It cost a lot of money.   **b** I didn't feel like it at all.
c It wasn't a problem.   **d** I was too scared to do it.
e I thought it was absolutely wonderful.
f No one told me anything.   **g** I'm very glad I did it.
h I had no idea.

Spelling

Correct the spelling of these words from Unit 5 by doubling one letter in each word.

1 acident   2 atitude   3 chalenge   4 comunity   5 eficient
6 sking   7 ster   8 straped   9 sudenly   10 suround
11 traveling   12 uncontrolably

Brainteaser

What comes once in a minute, twice in a moment, but never in an hour?

Answer on page 73.

UNIT 5

EXTENSION

LESSON 1

Think about what you've done today, and what you plan to do later on.

Write two sentences saying what you have just done.

....

....

Write two sentences saying what you have already done today.

....

....

Write two sentences saying what you haven't done yet.

....

....

LESSON 2

Write sentences about your experiences.

1 funny/film/see

   The funniest film I've ever seen is ...

2 nice/present/have

   ....

3 boring/book/read

   ....

4 good/song/hear

   ....

5 beautiful/place/visit

   ....

6 exciting/thing/do

   ....

LESSON 3

Correct the sentences.

1 He has won hundreds of medals ~~for~~ / *since* he was at school.
2 When have you had breakfast this morning?
3 I have wanted to be a doctor since over ten years.
4 How long did you have the jeans you're wearing?
5 We lived in this house since 2001.
6 They have bought a car yesterday.
7 My sister has know Lucy for five years.
8 How long have Mark had his car?

LESSON 4

What's the best experience you've ever had? Write a paragraph about it, saying when it happened, what happened, and why it's important to you.

....

....

....

....

....

....

Web watch

Search for 'Olympic Games' on the Internet and find out more about this important sports event. Look up new words in the dictionary and make a *Sports* section in your vocabulary notebook.

Spelling

Complete these adjectives with -*able* or -*ible*.

1 enjoy............   2 horr............   3 imposs............
4 incred............   5 invis............   6 memor............
7 miser............   8 respons............ 9 sens............
10 terr............   11 uncomfort............ 12 valu............

Brainteaser

Complete this sentence so that it is true.

The letter *e* appears ... times in this sentence.

Answer on page 73.

5 Culture

Tourism

1 Reading

Read the article *Responsible Tourism* and complete it with these words.

> animals   culture   environment   fair   groups   problems   respect   share   tourism   wild

RESPONSIBLE TOURISM

Holidays abroad are fun. But in many places tourists can cause real (1) _____, so more and more people are in favour of responsible tourism. This means (2) _____ where:

- tourists have an enjoyable holiday but also (3) _____ the place, the people and their culture.
- local people help make decisions about tourism and get a (4) _____ share of the money from it.
- there is as little damage to the (5) _____ as possible.

Examples of responsible tourism are:

- Community tourism, where small (6) _____ of tourists stay with local people in their villages. The tourists eat local food, see how the people live, and learn about their (7) _____.
- Ecotourism, where you stay in a (8) _____ environment like the rainforest and learn about its (9) _____ and plants. Ecotourism protects the environment and helps the local people who (10) _____ the money from it.

2 Reading

Read *Take action and have a better holiday!* on page 61. Then read the sentences and write *T* (true) or *F* (false). Correct the false sentences.

1 The clothes you wear may offend local people. ☐

2 Remember that the western way of doing things is always the best. ☐

3 You shouldn't take photos of people if they don't want you to. ☐

4 Giving sweets to children is a good idea. ☐

5 It's important that you pay as little as possible for the things that you buy. ☐

6 Don't ask the locals for advice on what to do and where to go. ☐

7 The further you fly, the better it is for the environment. ☐

Take action and have a better holiday!

❚❚ Be aware

Start thinking about your holiday before you leave. Think about what kind of clothes you should take. What kind of messages are you sending if you wear very little? What clothes do the locals wear?

❚❚ Be open

Something may seem strange to you, but it may be quite normal for the people who live in the country. Don't think that the 'western' way of doing things is always right.

❚❚ Our holidays, their homes

Ask before taking photos of people, even children, and respect their wishes. Talk to local people. What do they think about our lifestyle, clothes and ways of doing things? Find out about theirs.

❚❚ Pens, not sweets

Giving things like sweets to children makes them run after tourists. It's better to give things like pens or money to a local school or health centre.

❚❚ Be fair

Try to put money into local hands. If you bargain hard and pay as little as possible, you are not helping. Even if you pay a little more, does it really matter?

❚❚ Do your own thing

Use your guidebook or hotel as a starting point, but that's not the only way you can get information. Find out what's going on by talking to the locals and then do your own thing …

❚❚ Ask questions

Write an email to your tour company asking what they do about responsible tourism.

❚❚ Think before you fly

The more and the further you fly, the more you increase global warming and damage the environment.

3 Vocabulary

Match these words and phrases from the texts with their definitions.

1 abroad *adv* — a what someone wants
2 aware *adj* b how people live
3 be in favour of *v* c in other countries
4 do your own thing *v* d agree with
5 lifestyle *n* e knowing about something
6 protect *v* f part of something
7 responsible *adj* g do what you want to do
8 share *n* h keep something safe
9 wish *n* i thinking about the results of your actions

4 Reading

Read more of *The Tourists Are Coming* by Benjamin Zephaniah.

If by chance you see some
Try to make them welcome
　The tourists are coming
　The tourists are coming.

If they treat us good
They're welcome in the neighbourhood
　The tourists are coming
　The tourists are coming.

But if they're out of order
Show them to the border
　The tourists are coming
　The tourists are coming.

And if it does start raining
Tell them off if they're complaining
　The tourists are coming I say.

Tell them that we love living
And money can't buy everything
　The tourists are coming
　The tourists are coming.

What's the message of the poem to tourists?

5 Vocabulary

Make a word map for tourism.

6 Writing

Write a paragraph in your notebook about tourism in your country.

6 THAT'S CLEVER!

1 He had won awards

1 Reading

Read the article. Then match the beginnings of the sentences with the endings.

HAMSTER POWER

Night after night for several weeks, Elvis the hamster had kept the Ash family awake as he played on his wheel. But one evening, as he lay in bed listening to the hamster playing his favourite game, 16-year-old Peter Ash suddenly had a brilliant idea. 'Elvis was in his wheel for four or five hours a night and my sister Sarah complained that the noise kept her awake, so I thought it might as well do something good' said Peter. As part of a school science project, he invented a device to charge his mobile phone using the electricity created by the wheel. Peter's invention gave him 30 minutes of talk time on his phone for every two minutes that Elvis played on the wheel. The exercise was good for Elvis, and charging the phone this way was good for the environment. Peter had never invented anything before, but his hamster-powered phone charger helped him pass his electronics exam.

1 When Peter had his brilliant idea, ☐
2 For every two minutes that Elvis played on the wheel, ☐
3 Sarah had complained ☐
4 The hamster-powered phone charger was ☐
5 Using the wheel to charge Peter's phone was ☐
6 The inspiration for Peter's invention ☐

a the first thing Peter had ever invented.
b that the noise of the wheel kept her awake.
c Peter got 30 minutes of talk time on his mobile phone.
d was Elvis's favourite game.
e Elvis had kept the family awake for several weeks.
f good for Elvis and for the environment.

2 Past perfect

Write sentences in the past perfect.

1 It was my first visit to London – I/never go there before
   I'd never been there before.

2 He didn't know her – he/not meet her before
   ....

3 She didn't enjoy the film – she/already see it
   ....

4 They were late for the performance – it/already begin
   ....

5 There was no food left – they/eat everything on the table
   ....

6 He couldn't pay for the ticket – he/forget his wallet
   ....

7 She couldn't write to him – she/lose his address
   ....

8 She didn't have her bag – she/leave it on the bus
   ....

3 Past perfect

Answer the questions using these phrases in the past perfect.

> already read it   forget his keys   hear a good joke
> fail his exam   not hear the alarm clock
> ~~pass her driving test~~

1 Why was Lucia so happy?
   Because she'd passed her driving test.

2 Why was Dan late for work?
   ....
   ....

3 Why couldn't Michael get into the house?
   ....
   ....

UNIT 6

4 Why was Emma laughing?

5 Why was Tony depressed?

6 Why did Angela change the book?

4 Vocabulary

Match these words with their definitions.

| blind   deaf   disabled   sign language   slide v   workout |

1 activity to make your body stronger

2 move easily along something else

3 a … person is someone who can't see

4 a … person is someone who can't use part of their body or brain properly

5 a … person is someone who can't hear

6 deaf people can use this to communicate with each other

5 Vocabulary

Match the verbs in list A with the words and phrases in list B. Then write the phrases.

	A	B		
1	start	a glove	1	*start a business*
2	do	an idea	2	
3	recover	a sign	3	
4	make	exercises	4	
5	put on	your strength	5	
6	think of	a business	6	

6 Spelling

The same letter is missing in each line. Write the complete words.

1 sucessful   eletronics   bicyle

2 inspration   inventon   simplfy

3 advantag   ralise   soldir

4 disbled   balnce   languge

5 exerise   fasinated   sience

6 stregth   traslator   sig

7 Vocabulary

Match the words in list A with the words in list B and write five compound nouns.

	A	B		
1	swimming	food	1	*swimming pool*
2	computer	pool	2	
3	fast	language	3	
4	sign	out	4	
5	work	screen	5	

8 Pronunciation

Complete the chart with these words.

| appear   award   business   design   explain   invent
metal   product   soldier   system   translate   workout |

▪▫	▫▪
appear	

Extension Write a paragraph about what you did yesterday after you had got up.

63

6.2 THAT'S CLEVER!
People didn't use to throw things away

1 Reading

Read the text. Then read the sentences and write *T* (true) or *F* (false). Correct the false sentences.

The Mobius Loop

This symbol is called a 'mobius loop' and it is put on recycled products: things that used to be something else. The symbol shows the three parts of recycling: collecting material, turning it into something else, and selling it. People used to think that the only recycled product we could buy was paper, but that has changed entirely. In the past, recycled products often used to cost more, but this is no longer true – the more we buy, the cheaper recycled products get. And in the past people used to think recycled products weren't as good as products made from 'new' materials. Perhaps that used to be true, but it isn't now. So next time you go shopping, look for the mobius loop and come home with a bag which used to be a cap, or a mouse mat which used to be a car tyre!

1 You can find the mobius loop on products made from recycled materials. ☐

2 Recycled products used to be more expensive than new products. ☐

3 All recycled products are made of paper. ☐

4 Recycled products are still not as good as those made from new materials. ☐

5 It is not possible to recycle car tyres. ☐

2 *used to* + infinitive

Write sentences with *used to* + infinitive and these words.

aerobics instructor   diver   musician   painter   ~~pilot~~   soldier

1 *She used to be a pilot.*

2

3

4

5

6

UNIT 6

3 used to + infinitive

Write sentences using *used to* and *didn't use to*.

1 they/not recycle plastic bottles
  They didn't use to recycle plastic bottles, but they do now.

2 I/walk to school
  I used to walk to school, but I don't now.

3 People in the UK/not recycle much rubbish

4 she/drink coffee

5 we/play cards

6 my shoes/not wear out quickly

7 I/not send email

8 he/not like salsa

9 she/have long hair

4 Vocabulary

Match the items with the materials and write sentences using *made of*.

Items
a bicycle tyre   a book   a comb   gloves
knives and forks   shirts   tables

Materials
cotton   metal   paper   plastic   rubber   wood   wool

1 *A bicycle tyre is made of rubber.*
2
3
4
5
6
7

5 Vocabulary

Match the words in list A with the words in list B and write six compound nouns.

	A	B		
1	bottle	bottle	1	*bottle top*
2	vacuum	printer	2	
3	car	cleaner	3	
4	computer	pot	4	
5	hot water	top	5	
6	yoghurt	tyre	6	

6 Vocabulary

Match the verbs in list A with the words in list B. Then write the phrases.

	A	B		
1	mend	candles	1	*mend clothes*
2	play	clothes	2	
3	make	a letter	3	
4	light	cards	4	
5	make	phone calls	5	
6	write	a difference	6	

7 Vocabulary

Complete with these prepositions.

away   from   into   of   out

1 You can buy pencils made .... plastic cups.
2 Think before you throw something .... – perhaps you can recycle it.
3 In the past people used to use things until they wore ....
4 Car tyres are made .... rubber.
5 CDs can be turned .... bags.

8 Pronunciation

Do they rhyme (✔) or not (✘)?

1	twice	nice	✔
2	throw	now	
3	waste	fast	
4	tyre	fire	
5	wore	saw	
6	plant	want	
7	keys	cheese	
8	glass	gas	

Extension Write a paragraph about the differences between your life and your parents' lives when they were teenagers.

6 THAT'S CLEVER!

3 The first car was invented by him

1 Reading

Read and complete with the past simple passive of the verbs.

• FAMOUS WOMEN INVENTORS •

Dishwasher!

The world's first dishwasher (1) _____ (invent) by Josephine Cochran in 1886. It (2) _____ (demonstrate) at the 1893 World's Fair in Chicago. Cochran expected the machine to be popular with housewives, but it (3) _____ (buy) only by hotels and restaurants. It was not until the 1950s that dishwashers became popular with the general public.

Barbie!

The world's most famous doll (4) _____ (design) in 1959 by Ruth Handler, whose own daughter (5) _____ (call) Barbara. Barbie (6) _____ first _____ (see) at the American Toy Fair in New York. She was a great success and soon two Barbie dolls (7) _____ (sell) somewhere in the world every second.

Windscreen wiper!

In 1903, even before Henry Ford started making his famous Model A car, a device for cleaning a car windscreen (8) _____ (invent) by Mary Anderson. Her invention allowed drivers to clean rain or snow from the windscreen by using a handle inside the car. She wanted drivers to be able to see clearly even during bad weather.

Film star!

During the Second World War a secret communication system (9) _____ (develop) by Hollywood film star Hedy Lamarr. Messages (10) _____ (send) by radio in a secret code which the enemy could not read.

2 Past simple passive

Match the beginnings of the sentences with the endings. Then complete with the past simple passive.

1. People think that radio _____ (invent) by Marconi,
2. A new book suggests that Shakespeare wasn't the author of his plays,
3. Although the telephone _____ (develop) by Bell,
4. Madonna's single *Hung Up* uses part of *Gimme! Gimme! Gimme!*,
5. Although the first robot _____ (build) in the 1800s,
6. A Belgian, Leo Baekeland, who moved to the USA, invented plastic in 1909,
7. The first steam engine which went on rails _____ (build) by Richard Trevithick in 1808,
8. Leonardo da Vinci's car

a. which _____ (record) by Abba in 1979.
b. and, not surprisingly, it _____ (call) 'bakelite'.
c. _____ (power) by clockwork.
d. but that they _____ (write) by Sir Henry Neville.
e. they _____ (not use) in American factories until 1958.
f. but in fact radio waves _____ (discover) by Heinrich Hertz in 1887.
g. but the engines for the first world's first public railway _____ (make) by George Stephenson in 1825.
h. the real inventor of the phone was an Italian who _____ (call) Antonio Meucci.

UNIT 6

3 Past simple passive

Look at the picture and answer the questions using the past simple passive.

camel   dog   elephant   ~~lion~~   monkey   polar bear

1 Who attacked the policeman?

The policeman was attacked by the lion.

2 Who drove the car?

3 Who rode the bicycle?

4 Who trained the horses?

5 Who bit the snake?

6 Who ate the ice cream?

4 Vocabulary

Match the verbs in list A with the words and phrases in list B. Then write the phrases.

	A	B		
1	compose	a design	1	*compose music*
2	do	into practice	2	
3	run	damage	3	
4	put	music	4	
5	sketch	underwater	5	
6	swim	into something	6	

5 Vocabulary

Find eight words for jobs and occupations in the word square.

D	I	R	E	C	T	O	R	C
E	D	U	E	N	I	H	V	A
S	I	N	V	E	N	T	O	R
I	V	W	U	T	O	C	A	P
G	E	A	R	T	I	S	T	E
N	R	Y	P	U	P	N	I	N
E	N	G	I	N	E	E	R	T
R	S	O	L	D	I	E	R	E
A	R	F	K	N	O	O	R	R

6 Vocabulary

Match the words in list A with the words in list B and write five compound nouns.

	A	B		
1	light	jump	1	*light bulb*
2	short	alarm	2	
3	flying	list	3	
4	car	bulb	4	
5	parachute	machine	5	

7 Pronunciation

Say these words. Then cross out the silent letters.

bomb   built   design   highly   light   listener   thought   whether

8 Pronunciation

Complete the chart with these words.

~~atomic~~   carpenter   combustion   connection   designer   institute   internal   museum   powerful   replica   serious   vehicle

■■■	■■■
	atomic

Extension Write a paragraph about an inventor from your country and his/her most interesting invention.

67

6 THAT'S CLEVER!

4 Integrated Skills
Describing a process

1 Reading

Read and complete *My life story: from coffee plantation to cup* with these phrases.

a any bad beans were removed
b we were taken to a factory
c so that it was about three metres high
d put in the coffee machine
e which were white
f it cannot be grown in places where the temperature falls below zero
g put in bags
h to you, the customer
i so there was only one harvest that year

My life story: from coffee plantation to cup
by Mr Bean

Before you sit down and drink your next cup of coffee, think about me, Mr Bean, and my exciting journey from the plantations of Brazil to your cup.

I started life on a coffee tree, which was grown on a large farm, or plantation, in Brazil. The areas where coffee can be grown are all near to the Equator because the coffee tree is very sensitive. It needs heat, a lot of shade and regular but not constant rain, and (1) _____. About one third of the world's coffee is grown in Brazil.

Coffee trees can reach a height of 15 metres, but the top of my tree was cut off (2) _____. This made it easier to pick the coffee. My tree didn't flower until it was three years old. The flowers, (3) _____, lasted a few days. They then dropped off and coffee berries grew in their place. These coffee berries, which contained coffee beans, took ten months to ripen, (4) _____. The ripe berries were picked by hand and dried in the sun. The outer skin was then taken off, and all the beans, like me, came out into the sunlight for the first time.

Workers checked through us and (5) _____. I was put on the pile with the other good beans. We were then sorted according to size and (6) _____, ready to be taken to the market. At the market, we were sold to a coffee merchant. We were put in a warehouse and then taken by ship to the UK.

Next, (7) _____, where we were roasted: heated to a very high temperature and then cooled with water. When we were dry, we were put in bags again and sold to a coffee bar.

In the coffee bar, beans are ground (made into tiny pieces) and (8) _____. One kilo of beans will make between 80 and 100 cups of coffee. To make coffee, hot water is forced through the ground beans and poured into a cup. This is then sold (9) _____, and you can add milk and sugar if you want.

Think of me and my journey as you enjoy your coffee!

2 Number sentences A–H in the right order to show how the cup of coffee was produced.

A The beans were taken to the UK by ship. ☐
B The beans were sorted according to size. ☐
C The beans were ground in a coffee bar. ☐
D The beans were roasted. ☐
E The beans were sold to a merchant at the market. ☐
F The coffee beans were grown on a plantation in Brazil. ☐
G The ripe berries were picked. ☐
H The beans came out into the sunlight. ☐

3 Writing

Write short paragraphs in your notebook describing how the cup of coffee at the bar in the UK was produced. Structure your process description like this:

Brazil	First, ...
Market	Next, ...
Journey to the UK	Then ...
The factory	After that, ...
The coffee bar	Finally, ...
Your opinion	I think ...

4 Crossword

Complete the crossword.

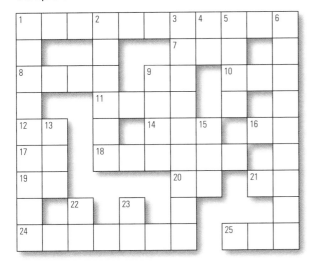

Across →

1 An ... person has new, different or exciting ideas. (11)
7 Braille uses ...s on paper. (3)
8 It's clever to ... plastic cups into pencils. (4)
9 Short for *television*. (2)
10 A chicken comes from this. (3)
11 Da Vinci came up with the ... for the first car. (4)
12 What you say if someone steps on your foot. (2)
14 Is there ... food left? (3)
16 The car was sketched by da Vinci ... 1478. (2)
17 If the tree falls, it could ... serious damage. (2)
18 Braille simplified Barbier's ... (6)
19 Short for *United Nations*. (2)
20 ... a child, Ryan was fascinated by electronics. (2)
21 Can you please help ...? (2)
24 I don't want them to ... a nuclear bomb. (7)
25 ... lamps were replaced by electric lights. (3)

Down ↓

1 Paper was ...d into Japan in AD 610. (9)
2 Someone who's brilliant like Leonardo da Vinci. (6)
3 Something extra which makes a thing or person better than others. (9)
4 Deaf people can use sign language ... communicate. (2)
5 Thing or object. (4)
6 People who design machines. (9)
9 'Four cups of tea, please.' or 'Four ..., please.' (4)
13 Past participle of *win*. (3)
15 Opposite of *no*. (3)
22 Opposite of *down*. (2)
23 We didn't use ... throw things away. (2)

UNIT 6

LEARNER INDEPENDENCE

Intensive reading skills

Intensive reading is what we do when we want to understand most or all of a text. Find techniques for being a good intensive reader by matching the instructions 1–6 with the questions a–f.

1 Look at the title. ☐
2 Read the text once quickly. ☐
3 Now read each paragraph of the text again slowly. ☐
4 Read again and underline any new words or expressions. ☐
5 Write sentences using each new word or expression you want to learn. ☐
6 Write a sentence giving your opinion of the text. ☐

a Which of the new words and expressions do you want to learn? Can you make up new sentences with them?
b What is each paragraph about? Can you think of a title for each paragraph?
c What is the main idea in the text?
d What did you think of the text? Was it enjoyable or interesting? Did you learn anything from it?
e Do you need to know the meaning of the new words or expressions? If you do, can you guess them before you look them up in a dictionary?
f What do you think the text is going to be about?

Extensive reading

Read *Robinson Crusoe* and choose a picture which you like. Write a paragraph describing what is in the picture, saying what happened just before the event in the picture and what happened after.

The young Robinson Crusoe ignores his father's advice and decides to become a sailor. But Crusoe is soon caught up in violent storms and finds himself shipwrecked on a remote island where he must live for the next 28 years.

6 THAT'S CLEVER!
Inspiration EXTRA!

REVISION

LESSON 1

Complete using the past perfect of these verbs.

> change   forget   ~~get~~   go   invent   see   win

1 When he didn't recognise the buildings he realised that he ___had got___ lost.
2 I _____ never _____ them before, so I didn't know what they looked like.
3 They were really happy because they _____ the game.
4 After he left the party, he realised that he _____ his jacket.
5 Amos, Patterson, Morlan and Braille _____ all _____ things before they were 18.
6 I _____ not _____ to the beach for years and was surprised by how much it _____.

LESSON 2

Complete using *used to* or *didn't use to* and these words and phrases.

> be allowed   be possible   ~~bother~~   drive   recycle   turn off

1 People ___didn't use to bother___ about recycling, but now they do.
2 People _____ to smoke in public places in the UK, but now they aren't.
3 It _____ to film a video with a phone, but now it is.
4 She _____ a car, but now she cycles or goes by bus.
5 They _____ the lights when they left a room, but now they do.
6 People _____ all their waste during the Second World War.

LESSON 3

Write sentences using the past simple passive.

1 colour television/invent/1904/a German
   ___Colour television was invented in 1904 by a German.___
2 first BBC television show/broadcast/1929
   _____
3 first TV interview/hold/April 1930
   _____
4 first TV play/show/July 1930
   _____
5 first horse race which/see/on TV was The Derby/1931
   _____

LESSON 4

Match these words with their definitions.

1 approximately   ☐
2 complicated   ☐
3 connect   ☐
4 supply   ☐
5 plastic surgery ☐
6 process   ☐

a provide what is needed or wanted
b join two things together
c difficult to do or understand
d series of actions
e opposite of *exactly*
f operation to improve someone's appearance

Spelling

Correct the spelling of these words from Unit 6 by doubling one letter in each word.

1 aproximately   2 atempt   3 botle   4 conect
5 endles   6 enginer   7 ful-scale   8 posibility
9 proces   10 self-propeled   11 suply   12 suporter

Brainteaser

What makes a pair of shoes?

Answer on page 73.

UNIT 6

EXTENSION

LESSON 1

Why did these things happen? Use the phrases in the box or your own ideas and write answers in the past perfect.

> borrow her mother's car without asking
> ~~leave his books at school~~   fall into the swimming pool
> forget which day it was   promise not to be late
> see Carl fall off his chair   spend it all in the café
> go to the cinema with Tara

1 Why didn't Franco have any homework?
  Because he'd left his books at school.

2 Why was Ruth's dress wet?

3 Why didn't Alberto have any money?

4 Why was Dan so pleased with himself?

5 Why was Emilia in trouble?

6 Why was Tara in such a hurry?

7 Why was Susanna laughing?

8 Why didn't Franz go to the party?

LESSON 2

Write three sentences using *used to* or *didn't use to* about yourself, and three about a friend.

I didn't use to like ballet, but now I do.

LESSON 3

Write questions and answer them.

1 Books: who/write by
  Who was the 'Twilight' series written by?
  Stephenie Meyer.

2 Music: who/record by

3 Film: who/direct by

4 Film: who/play by/in (*film*)

5 Invention: who/invent by

6 Discovery: who/discover by

LESSON 4

Write a short paragraph saying which inventions in *Ancient Inventions* on page 80 of the Student's Book are the most important and why.

Web watch

Search the Internet for one of the teenage inventors from Lesson 1 or Leonardo da Vinci from Lesson 3 and find out more about them. Make an *Inventors* section in your vocabulary notebook.

Spelling

Read and complete the words from Unit 6.

The combination of sounds /ʃən/ is usually spelled *-tion*:
communication   connec_____   inspira_____
instruc_____   inven_____

The combination of sounds /stʃən/ is usually spelt *-stion*:
question   sugge_____   combu_____

Note: /ʃən/ politician   permission   /ʒən/ television

Brainteaser

What does someone have to take before you can get it?
Answer on page 73.

REVIEW
UNITS 5–6

1 Read and complete. For each number 1–14, choose word or phrase A, B, C or D.

AFRICAN DREAM

SUNDAY
I was dreaming. My horse had just won the Grand National – the biggest horse race of the year in Britain. And I had won over £100. I couldn't believe it – I (**1**) _____ so much money before. I opened my eyes and closed them again quickly. My head (**2**) _____. But it wasn't a dream. My horse had won the race and I had won all that money. And spent it. My friends and I (**3**) _____ all night, and I'd had (**4**) _____ to eat and drink, and no sleep. I felt terrible.

I opened my eyes again and saw a big green thing in the middle of my room. Suddenly I remembered and sat up quickly in bed. The green thing was my rucksack. It was (**5**) _____ packed. Today was the day for me to fly to Africa to join my friends. I (**6**) _____ dream about travelling in southern Africa and had worked (**7**) _____ six months to save money for this trip. I was 18 and was going to university in the autumn. Today was the start of the dream, but I felt like death. I couldn't eat or drink anything on the flight, or at the airport in Abu Dhabi where I changed planes.

MONDAY
In Johannesburg I was the first person in the baggage hall. And the last. 'I'm sorry, sir, your rucksack (**8**) _____ put on the plane in Abu Dhabi,' I (**9**) _____. So here I was at the start of my African dream – no rucksack and no clothes.

TUESDAY
I was staying at a backpackers' hostel and things soon got better. I met a nice guy called Mike at the hostel – he was from the same town as me, but we'd (**10**) _____ met before! Strange! We went out to listen to a band in the evening. We waited and waited, but no band. So we (**11**) _____ pool in the bar. At 11 o'clock the band started to play the most fantastic music. And the guitarist was one of the guys we (**12**) _____ pool with! It was a great experience, not only the music, but also the colourful clothes and the way the audience took part.

WEDNESDAY
Mike took me out to the airport in his car. They (**13**) _____ my rucksack – in Abu Dhabi. My friends were in Bulawayo in Zimbabwe, so I asked the airline to send the rucksack there.

THURSDAY
I took the bus for Bulawayo at 6.30 in the morning. The journey took nine hours and I tried to sleep. When I woke up, the bus had stopped at a petrol station. In many ways it looked just like Europe. But suddenly a giraffe (**14**) _____ across the road in front of the bus.

FRIDAY
Today I went out to Bulawayo Airport. There, in the baggage hall, going round and round on its own, was my lovely green rucksack. My African dream was beginning – five days late!

	A	B	C	D
1	never win	never won	had never won	had ever won
2	hurt	hurts	has hurt	had hurt
3	celebrated	celebrate	have celebrated	had celebrated
4	too	too much	too many	too few
5	ever	never	already	just
6	used to	use to	'm used to	used
7	in	for	from	since
8	isn't	wasn't	hasn't	hadn't
9	told	is told	am telling	was told
10	ever	never	already	just
11	play	have played	played	had played
12	play	have played	are playing	had played
13	find	have found	found	had found
14	walk	have walked	walked	had walked

2 Use the word in capitals to form a word for each space.

1 He found the task _____ because he hadn't done it before. CHALLENGE
2 Her _____ increased after she was in a reality TV show. POPULAR
3 The restaurant's _____ is lobster. SPECIAL
4 Louis Braille was the _____ of the universal alphabet for blind people. INVENT
5 There's a _____ between air travel and global warming. CONNECT
6 The overnight flight to South Africa seemed _____. END
7 There's a _____ that you are wrong. POSSIBLE
8 Sports cars have very _____ engines. POWER

3 Complete the second sentence so that it means the same as the first sentence. Use the word in bold without changing it.

1 The film started a few minutes ago. **already**
  The film _____
2 This is the first time he'll try ski-jumping. **never**
  He has _____
3 My parents got married 20 years ago. **for**
  My parents _____
4 She left the party before he arrived. **after**
  He arrived _____
5 We don't have lunch together on Sunday any more. **to**
  We _____
6 The Europeans didn't discover chocolate until 1519. **by**
  Chocolate _____

4 Find the odd word.

1 leather paper rubber runner
2 helicopter explorer interviewer soldier
3 bus car lorry vehicle
4 cotton denim glass wool
5 award race medal prize
6 bag cup brick pot

Answers to Brainteasers

UNIT 5
Revision the letter *m*
Extension ten

UNIT 6
Revision two shoes
Extension a photo

LEARNER INDEPENDENCE
SELF ASSESSMENT

Vocabulary

1 Draw this chart in your notebook. How many words can you write in each category?

More than 10? Good! *More than 12?* Very good!
More than 15? Excellent!

Sport	
Materials	
Household items	

2 Put the words in order to make expressions from the phrasebooks in Lesson 4 in Units 5 and 6.

1 clue have didn't a I
  I didn't have a clue.
2 wondered like ever you have what it's
3 it matter really didn't
4 it let's stays hope way that
5 was worth well it it
6 endless possibilities the are
7 not or it believe
8 well really doing it's

Check your answers.
8/8 Excellent! *6/8* Very good! *4/8* Try again!

My learning diary
In Units 5 and 6:
My favourite topic is _____

My favourite picture is _____

The three lessons I like most are _____

My favourite activity or exercise is _____

Something I don't understand is _____

Something I want to learn more about is _____

73

7 COMMUNICATION

1 He asked her not to go

1 Reading

Read and complete the text with these words.

> apes asked communicate driver language
> memory number parrot picture remarkable
> talk teach verbs vocabulary words

N'kisi – the psychic parrot

Scientists are amazed by the (1) _____ talents of an African grey parrot called N'kisi. The bird is believed to be one of the best users of human (2) _____ in the animal world. N'kisi has a (3) _____ of 950 words and he can (4) _____ in sentences. He uses (5) _____ with past, present and future tenses and he also makes up (6) _____ and phrases when he needs to. N'kisi doesn't just (7) _____ – his owner and Aimee Morgan, uses picture cards to (8) _____ him to read.

Even more amazing is the fact that N'kisi can apparently read people's minds! In an experiment, Aimee looked at a (9) _____ of photos in one room, while N'kisi was filmed and recorded in another room. When Aimee looked at a (10) _____ of two people hugging, N'kisi (11) _____ 'Can I give you a hug?' and when she looked at a photo of a (12) _____ with his head out of the car window, the (13) _____ said 'Uh-oh, careful, you put your head out.'

N'kisi also has a good (14) _____ – when he met the chimpanzee expert Dr Jane Goodall, after seeing her in a photo with (15) _____, his first words to her were: 'Got a chimp?'

2 ask/tell + object + infinitive

Write sentences reporting the requests with *asked* and the commands with *told*.

1 What did the man say to the woman?

He asked her to pass the salt.

3 What did the police officer say to the driver?

2 What did the woman say to the boys?

4 What did the young man say to the old lady?

UNIT 7

You have to work harder and run faster.

5 What did the coach say to the team?

You mustn't touch anything.

6 What did the guard say to the girls?

Can you open your mouth wide, please?

7 What did the doctor say to the man?

3 Vocabulary

Complete with these verbs.

come   go   make   pick   put   stand   take (x2)   turn

1 Don't leave your books on the floor – _____ them up!

2 You'd better _____ off your dirty shoes.

3 He'd broken his leg, so he couldn't _____ up.

4 If you're cold, you can _____ on a sweater.

5 I don't believe that story – did you _____ it up?

6 I'm trying to finish homework – please _____ away.

7 Don't _____ my plate away. I haven't finished eating yet.

8 _____ off the tap so you don't waste water.

9 As we were leaving, our grandmother told us to _____ back soon.

4 Vocabulary

Find these wild animals in the word square.

1 It lives in South America and has a long neck.
2 It's a small ape.
3 It's a large ape.
4 It has black and yellow-brown stripes.
5 It has black and white stripes.
6 It's a large mammal that lives in the sea.
7 It's a large fish with lots of teeth.
8 It's a large reptile with lots of teeth.
9 It's a large African cat.
10 It looks like a large dog.
11 It's a tropical bird.

M	W	O	L	F	C	N	U	T	L	K
I	B	R	L	H	P	A	L	I	O	N
X	W	F	A	D	G	Q	Y	G	I	Z
C	H	I	M	P	A	N	Z	E	E	E
P	A	F	A	A	S	L	T	R	M	B
O	L	Y	R	R	B	P	S	O	W	R
A	E	G	O	R	I	L	L	A	V	A
H	I	C	R	O	C	O	D	I	L	E
X	C	P	D	T	S	H	A	R	K	L

5 Pronunciation

Say these words. Then cross out the silent letters.

brou~~gh~~t   building   calm   guilty   often   sign   taught

6 Pronunciation

Do they rhyme (✔) or not (✘)?

1	clearly	really	✔
2	fine	sign	☐
3	grey	key	☐
4	brought	taught	☐
5	centre	enter	☐
6	splash	wash	☐
7	bird	word	☐
8	rude	should	☐

Extension Write four things that you have asked people to do or not to do recently. Make one of them false. Read them out to another student. Can they guess which is false?

75

7.2 COMMUNICATION
He said he couldn't remember

1 Reading

Read and complete the text with these words.

asked   autumn   communication   engineer
had   inventor   messages   programs
remember   said   thought   was

It wasn't a very exciting message. But the single phrase QWERTYUIOP marked a communications breakthrough, because it was the first email … perhaps. Ray Tomlinson, the (1) _____ of email, isn't 100% sure. He (2) _____, 'I sent a number of test (3) _____ from one machine to another. They were all entirely forgettable.'

Ray can't even (4) _____ the exact date – it was some time in the (5) _____ of 1971. At the time, he was chief (6) _____ at a technology company in the USA. He was developing a (7) _____ system which linked computers together. He said he (8) _____ simply combined two computer (9) _____ to create the first email.

At first, Ray didn't realise that his invention (10) _____ so important. In fact, he even (11) _____ one of his colleagues to keep quiet about it, in case people (12) _____ he was wasting time at work!

Now read the sentences and write *T* (true) or *F* (false). Correct the false sentences.

1 The phrase QWERTYIUIOP was not very important. ☐

2 The test messages were easy to forget. ☐

3 The first email was created by separating two programs. ☐

4 Ray knew that his invention was important. ☐

5 Ray asked one of his colleagues not to tell anyone about his invention. ☐

6 Ray was worried people would think he was wasting his time. ☐

2 Reported statements

Report what the speakers said.

1 'I want to go to university,' said Sophie.
   Sophie said that she wanted to go to university.

2 Jess said, 'Not everyone can sing like a star.'

3 'I'm trying to do revision for my exams,' said Rob.

4 Anna said, 'I really don't like pizza so I refuse to eat it.'

5 'I don't want to panic, but I'm really worried about my best friend,' said Lara.

6 Maxim said, 'They've found Rebecca.'

7 'I heard someone walking around my room,' said Janet.

8 The free-runner said, 'I've never done anything like it before!'

9 'Tomorrow we're going to Lake Titicaca,' said Julie.

10 Rob said, 'I'll walk home – I've just missed the last bus.'

UNIT 7

3 Reported statements

Report these famous quotations.

1 'Freedom is not worth having if it does not include the freedom to make mistakes.'
Mahatma Gandhi

Mahatma Gandhi said that freedom was not worth having if it didn't include the freedom to make mistakes.

2 'History is the version of past events that people have decided to agree upon.' **Napoleon Bonaparte**

3 'You can live to be a hundred if you give up all the things that make you want to live to be a hundred.' **Woody Allen**

4 'I can't understand why a person will take a year to write a novel when he can easily buy one for a few dollars.' **Fred Allen**

5 'Whenever people agree with me, I always feel I must be wrong.' **Oscar Wilde**

6 'There's only one way to have a happy marriage and as soon as I learn what it is, I'll get married again.' **Clint Eastwood**

7 'Television has proved that people will look at anything rather than each other.' **Ann Landers**

8 'When they discover the centre of the universe, a lot of people will be disappointed to discover they are not it.' **Bernard Bailey**

9 'The time to repair the roof is when the sun is shining.' **John F Kennedy**

4 Vocabulary

Complete with the correct form of *say* or *tell*.

1 You can't go in there – the sign _____ 'No entry'.
2 Excuse me, can you _____ me the time?
3 The children were quiet when the teacher _____ them a story.
4 Please could you _____ that again.
5 I'll _____ you a secret, but you mustn't repeat it.
6 'Promise to work together,' _____ Adam.
7 If you see Rob, _____ hello to him from me.
8 Maxim _____ his wife to change her clothes.
9 It's very important to _____ the truth.
10 It _____ on the radio that it was going to rain today.

5 Vocabulary

Match the words in list A with the words in list B and write six compound words.

	A	B	
1	computer	attachment	1 *computer file*
2	user	through	2
3	email	name	3
4	social	file	4
5	break	wide	5
6	world	networking	6

6 Vocabulary

Find words or phrases in the text on page 90 of the Student's Book which match these definitions.

1 quite cross _____
2 way to solve a problem _____
3 difficult _____
4 remove, take out _____
5 recall _____

7 Pronunciation

Mark the stressed syllable.

■
attachment   communicate   effect   exchange
interviewer   program   provider   service   solution   virus

> **Extension** Write a paragraph in your notebook saying how often you use your email account and your online profile. What do you use each one for?

7 COMMUNICATION

3 They asked how he had got the idea

1 Reading

Read the interview with an alien. Then complete the interviewer's report using reported speech.

INTERVIEWER	Where do you come from?
ALIEN	I'm from a planet called Astra.
INTERVIEWER	How long have you been here?
ALIEN	I arrived six months ago.
INTERVIEWER	Why did you come here?
ALIEN	I want to write a book about life on Earth.
INTERVIEWER	Where are you staying?
ALIEN	I'm staying at a hotel in New York.
INTERVIEWER	Do you like New York?
ALIEN	I think it's an amazing city.
INTERVIEWER	Are you happy about being the centre of media attention?
ALIEN	I don't like people taking photos of me.

I asked the alien where he had come from. He said he was from a planet called Astra.

2 Reported questions

Match the reported questions with the pictures and write them in direct speech.

a She asked him if he liked her hair.
b He asked her if they could have two tickets.
c She asked him which street he was looking for.
d ~~She asked him how much the jeans were.~~
e He asked her if she had seen his trainers.
f He asked her when she had last had her bag.

1. How much are the jeans?

2.

3.

4.

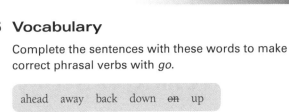

3 Reported questions

Write the questions in reported speech.

1 SOPHIE 'Rob, what time is it?'
   Sophie asked Rob what time it was.

2 ROB 'Dad, can you lend me some money?'

3 LORNA 'Why did you decide to come to *Star School*, Nick?'

4 DAVE 'Rob, how long have you lived in north London?'

5 ANNA 'Do you like hip-hop, Will?'

6 POLICE OFFICER 'Janet, have you ever seen a ghost?'

7 SIMON 'Do you know where we're going, Julie?'

8 INTERVIEWER 'Ewan and Charley, what are you going to do next?'

4 Vocabulary

Match the words in list A with the words in list B and write five compound nouns.

A	B		
1 secondary	interest	1	*secondary school*
2 wind	mill	2	
3 school	school	3	
4 car	fees	4	
5 media	parts	5	

5 Vocabulary

Complete the sentences with these words to make correct phrasal verbs with *go*.

ahead away back down ~~on~~ up

1 It started snowing in the morning, and it went ___*on*___ all day.

2 William went _____ to school after his TV interview.

3 'Can we start eating?' – 'Yes, of course, go _____.'

4 She's feeling much better because her temperature has gone _____.

5 In most places the temperature goes _____ during the day.

6 It's been a month since he went _____ and we really miss him.

6 Pronunciation

Write these words under *dog* or *month*, according to the pronunciation of the underlined letters.

~~bec<u>o</u>me~~ bl<u>o</u>gger b<u>o</u>rrow cr<u>o</u>ps c<u>ou</u>ntry d<u>o</u>ne d<u>o</u>zen
dr<u>o</u>p g<u>o</u>ne m<u>o</u>ney sch<u>o</u>larship s<u>ou</u>thern st<u>o</u>ck w<u>o</u>n

/ɒ/ dog	/ʌ/ month
	become

7 Pronunciation

Write the number of syllables and mark the stress.

borrowed _2_   central ____   disease ____

electricity ____   media ____   phenomenal ____

remarkable ____   scholarship ____   starvation ____

> **Extension** Use six of the words in exercise 7 to write sentences. Try to use reported speech.

7 COMMUNICATION

4 Integrated Skills
Telling a story

1 Reading

Read *The War of the Worlds* and number paragraphs A–E in the right order.

THE WAR OF THE WORLDS

A _____

As a result, American people started to panic, particularly in New Jersey and New York. Many jumped into their cars (**1**) _____. Some rushed out of their houses with wet cloths over their faces (**2**) _____. Others picked up their guns and started moving household furniture. Thousands of terrified people called the police, newspaper offices and radio stations (**3**) _____.

B _____

On the evening of 30 October 1938, between 8.15 and 9.30pm, millions of Americans turned on their radios to listen to a play based on H G Wells' novel *The War of the Worlds*. This famous science fiction story is about Martians (**4**) _____. But American director Orson Welles moved the action to the United States and presented his radio play as a realistic news broadcast with dramatic sound effects.

C _____

Afterwards, Orson Welles said he was very sorry (**5**) _____. He added that he hadn't been sure about presenting *The War of the Worlds* because people might be bored or annoyed (**6**) _____. But Welles' play is probably the most successful radio drama in history.

D _____

The news broadcast and sound effects were so realistic that large numbers of listeners thought they were hearing an account of an actual Martian attack. First, they heard news reports that a huge burning object had fallen (**7**) _____. Then an actor playing a reporter described the aliens coming out of their spaceship. He said they were enormous grey monsters, (**8**) _____.

E _____

By the end of the evening, the police had managed to spread the message (**9**) _____. When the American public realised what had happened, many people were extremely angry and complained about the broadcast. The power of mass communications had made people believe things that weren't true.

Now complete the text with these phrases.

- **a** with horrible faces and black eyes
- **b** and asked how they could protect themselves
- **c** landing on Earth and attacking Britain
- **d** and the roads were soon filled with traffic
- **e** that his dramatic broadcast had caused so much panic
- **f** that the Martian attack was imaginary
- **g** on a farm in New Jersey
- **h** to escape from poisonous Martian gas
- **i** by such an unlikely story

80

UNIT 7

2 Complete this summary of the story using information from the completed text.

In the science fiction novel *The War of the Worlds*, Martians _____.
Orson Welles' 1938 play was set in the USA and sounded like _____. First,
listeners heard on the radio that _____. Then they heard a description of
_____. There was enormous panic in _____. People
called the police because _____. Many people complained about the broadcast when
_____. Later, Orson Welles apologised for _____.

3 Crossword

Complete the crossword.

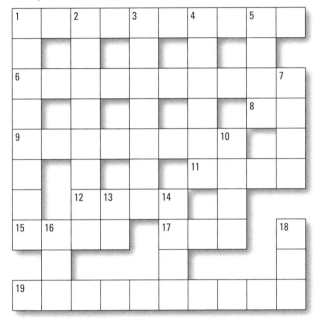

Across →
1. Intelligent African animal – Kanzi is one. (10)
6. Extraordinary or extremely surprising. (10)
8. Singular of *us*. (2)
9. We use this computer system to send emails. (8)
11. Opposite of *alive*. (4)
12. Noun formed from *famous*. (4)
15. Monday and Tuesday are ... of the week. (4)
17. Animal doctor. (3)
19. Someone who does research. (10)

Down ↓
1. Ken and Emily were thrown into the sea when their dinghy ... (8)
2. Alex the parrot could ... shapes, colours and materials. (8)
3. A virus is a computer ... which damages or destroys information. (7)
4. William built a windmill because his village ... electricity. (6)
5. Important test at school or university. (4)
7. Opposite of *borrow*. (4)
10. You can send ... messages from a mobile phone. (4)
13. Kanzi makes up words, such ... 'white tiger' (zebra). (2)
14. Have you ... phoned the emergency number? (4)
16. A gorilla is a member of the ... family. (3)
18. How ... is Japan from the UK? About 10,000 km. (3)

LEARNER INDEPENDENCE

Telling a story

When we tell a news story, we usually summarise the facts and say what we think about the event. Find an interesting news story (on a website, on the radio/TV, in a newspaper) and make notes answering these questions:

- When and where did the event happen?
- What happened?
- Why did it happen? Do you know?
- What was the result?
- How did other people respond to the event? What did they say?
- What's your response to the event – what do you think about it?

Now tell another student about the news story.

Extensive reading

Read *Pride and Prejudice*, which is one of the most famous English novels.

Now draw a simple picture of a scene or character from the book (not a copy of a picture in the book). Give your picture a title. Then show it to another student and answer his/her questions about what your picture shows and why you chose it. (*Who ...? What ...? When ...? Where ...? Why ...?*)

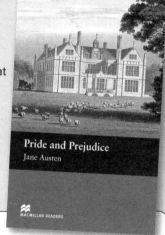

Mrs Bennet has five daughters and she wants to find husbands for them all. When a rich young man – Mr Bingley – comes to live at Netherfield Hall, Mrs Bennet is delighted. He will be the perfect husband for her eldest daughter, Jane. Mr Bingley arrives at Netherfield Hall with a friend, Mr Darcy, who is very rich, very handsome – and extremely proud. Elizabeth Bennet, the second daughter, is attractive, intelligent and lively. She dislikes Mr Darcy immediately.

7 COMMUNICATION
Inspiration EXTRA!

REVISION

LESSON 1

Write sentences reporting the teacher's requests with *asked* and the commands with *told*.

1 'Robert, could you open the window, please?'
   She asked Robert to open the window.

2 'Sara and Maria, don't talk!'

3 'Open your books, everyone.'

4 'Pedro, please would you clean the board?'

5 'Sara and Maria, stop laughing!'

6 'Daniel, can you share your book with Anna?'

7 'Anna, please don't forget your book tomorrow.'

8 'Now, everyone, listen to me carefully.'

LESSON 2

Write what the people said in direct speech.

1 Ray said that he couldn't remember the exact date.
   'I can't remember the exact date.'

2 Rob said that he was looking forward to his birthday.

3 Sophie said that she went to parties every Saturday night.

4 Joni said that she had fallen asleep on the beach.

5 Jess said that she would teach the contestants to sing.

6 Anna said that she didn't like pizza.

7 Richard said there were thousands of silly laws in the USA.

8 Maxim said that they had to drive back to Manderley.

LESSON 3

Put the words in order to make reported questions.

1 what my asked she number was phone

2 wanted film when they started know the to

3 asked much I the cost bike how

4 were where the asked teacher going students the

5 if team won to he know his wanted had

6 stopped the had car why asked we

LESSON 4

Complete the questions for these answers about Ken and Emily's sailing accident.

1 Where
   They were sailing near Southampton.

2 Why
   Because their dinghy capsized in huge waves.

3 Where
   It was in her pocket.

4 Who
   Ken and Emily's father did.

5 When
   About ten minutes later.

6 What
   He said the teenagers were lucky to be alive.

Spelling

Correct the spelling of these words from Unit 7 by doubling one letter in each word.

1 atachment 2 atention 3 atract 4 borow 5 busines
6 bloger 7 comand 8 comunicate 9 corectly 10 windmil

Brainteaser

What should you keep after you've given it to someone else?

Answer on page 97.

UNIT 7

EXTENSION

LESSON 1

Write sentences describing the pictures using *asked/told* + object + infinitive.

1

2

3

4

5

6

LESSON 2

Correct the sentences.

1 Ray said it had probably ~~took~~ *taken* four to six hours to invent email.
2 Sophie said she has never enjoyed herself so much.
3 The professor told the car was a very powerful machine.
4 Usain said that NJ was still her best friend in the world.
5 Ken and Emily said they can't attract the attention of passing ships.
6 Ken told Emily they will have to call the coastguard.
7 Mrs Danvers said she was liking the picture of the girl in white.
8 Rob said her that he was trying to do revision for his exams.

LESSON 3

Ask another student questions about their last holiday and note down the answers. Then write sentences reporting the questions and answers.

I asked Barbara when her last holiday was. She said that ...

LESSON 4

Think about a dramatic event in your life. Write a paragraph about it, saying when and where it happened, what the result was, and how you felt about it.

Web watch

Do you want to revise your Internet skills? Search the Internet for 'Internet Skills' and take a free course.

What did you learn? Make an *Internet* section in your vocabulary notebook.

Spelling

Complete the words with *ie* or *ei*. How many different sounds do they represent?

1 bel___ve   2 b___ng   3 carr___d   4 ___ther
5 f___ld   6 fr___ndly 7 h___ght   8 interv___w
9 qu___t   10 rec___ve 11 repl___d
12 sc___nce 13 soc___ty 14 w___ght

Brainteaser

It's faster than the speed of light.
It's darker than the darkest night.
When something is free, you pay it.
When you have a shower, you wear it.
When you lose, you win it.
When you're silent, you say it.
Poor people have it.
Rich people need it.
If you eat it, you'll die.
What is it?

Answer on page 97.

7 Culture

Global English

English Fact File

What does the word *English* mean? The answer is surprising – it means 'fish hook'! The English people and language take their name from the Angles. The Angles travelled to England from southern Denmark and northern Germany 1,500 years ago. They came from a place called Angul, which looked like a fish hook, and *Angul* slowly became *English*.

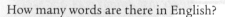

How many words are there in English?

A 10,000   B 100,000   C At least 1,000,000.
D No one knows.

The correct answer is D because the language is constantly growing. But C is also true – there are over a million words in English.

In Shakespeare's time, only five to seven million people spoke English, and they all lived in Britain. Then, in the 1620s, people from Britain emigrated to North America and took the English language with them. Today there are around 60 million English-speakers in Britain, but more than 250 million people speak English in the USA and Canada!

- 85% of international organisations use English as one of their working languages, 49% use French and under 10% use Arabic, German or Spanish.
- 99% of European organisations use English as one of their working languages, 63% use French and 40% German.
- 42% of EU citizens can communicate in English, 31% in German and 29% in French.
- Over 70% of European satellite TV viewers can understand the news in English and 40% in French or German.

William Caxton printed the first book in English in 1475. In Caxton's time different people spelt words in different ways. Caxton himself spelt *please* sometimes *plese* and sometimes *playse*. The first dictionary appeared in 1604 but it only contained about 3,000 words. It wasn't until 100 years later that everyone agreed on how to spell English words. Unfortunately, it is often impossible to guess the pronunciation of words from the spelling. For example, compare the pronunciation of *gh* in *laugh*, *ghost* and *through*! And what about the pronunciation of *o* in *won*, *woman* and *women*?

There are at least 1,500 million speakers of English in the world.
- English as a first language is spoken in countries such as the USA, the UK, Canada, Australia and New Zealand. Each of these countries has its own variety of English with its own pronunciation and different vocabulary.
- English as a second language is spoken by over 375 million people in countries like India, in East and West Africa, and in south-east Asia. These areas also have their own varieties of English and use the language in administration, business and education.
- English as a foreign language is spoken by more than 750 million people, who learn it in school and use it to communicate with people from other countries.

Languages are dying! Now that more and more people speak English, what is going to happen to the other languages in the world? In 1966, there were 6,703 languages in the world. Scientists think that by the end of the 21st century 50% of these will be extinct, and another 40% will be in danger. So, although we can use English for international communication, we should protect our own languages at home.

1 Reading

Read the *English Fact File* and write questions for these answers.

1 _____
   At least 1,500 million.
2 _____
   In the 1620s.
3 _____
   6,703.
4 _____
   Only five million.
5 _____
   In 1475.
6 _____
   More than 750 million.
7 _____
   99% of them.
8 _____
   1,500 years ago.

2 Vocabulary

Match these words from the text with their definitions.

1 administration *n* ☐
2 citizens *n pl* ☐
3 constantly *adv* ☐
4 contained *v* ☐
5 emigrated *v* ☐
6 extinct *adj* ☐
7 growing *v* ☐
8 hook *n* ☐
9 variety *n* ☐
10 viewers *n pl* ☐

a getting bigger
b small piece of bent metal used for catching fish
c left to live in another country
d all the time
e specific kind
f what managers have to run in organisations
g dead, no longer existing
h people watching TV
i had inside
j people who live in a town or country

3 Vocabulary

Thousands of words in English are borrowed from other languages. Can you match these words with the languages they come from?

Languages
French   German   Greek   Italian   Polish   Spanish

1 ballet _____
2 banana _____
3 chocolate _____
4 cinema _____
5 delicatessen _____
6 giraffe _____
7 guitar _____
8 hamburger _____
9 hippo _____
10 hotel _____
11 polka _____
12 microphone _____
13 mosquito _____
14 opera _____
15 parachute _____
16 piano _____
17 restaurant _____
18 rhino _____
19 tornado _____
20 violin _____

4 Pronunciation

Find words in the *English Fact File* which rhyme with these words but have a different spelling.

1 dancer _____
2 half _____
3 heard _____
4 news _____
5 phone _____
6 rule _____
7 shoe _____
8 turn _____
9 worst _____

5 Writing

There are many good reasons for learning foreign languages. Write a paragraph saying why English will be useful to you in the future.

_____
_____
_____
_____

85

8 NATURAL WORLD

1 They should have thought ...

1 Reading

Read the text and complete the sentences below it with *should have* or *shouldn't have* and suitable verbs.

This is Mr Gas Guzzler. He has just used up the last litre of petrol in the world. He doesn't have a family, but last year he bought a large car. The car didn't get very dirty, but he washed it every day. Although he had a bike, he didn't use it very often. He lives quite close to the shops but he always drove there, he never walked. When he went on long journeys he always drove, he never took the train. He didn't care about the environment – he only cared about having fun.

1 He _shouldn't have bought_ a large car.
  He _should have bought_ a small one.

2 He _____ it every day.
  He _____ it once a month.

3 He _____ his bike more.
  He _____ his car less.

4 He _____ to the shops.

5 For long journeys, he _____ by car. He _____ the train.

6 He _____ more about the environment. He _____ less about his own fun.

2 should(n't) have

Write sentences using *should have* or *shouldn't have*.

1 pack so many clothes

She shouldn't have packed so many clothes.

2 measure the table before he bought it

3 buy a ticket

4 forget her umbrella

5 believe everything the salesman said

6 think of the consequences

7 be rude to the referee

8 turn the taps off

UNIT 8

3 ought(n't) to have

Write sentences using *ought to have* or *oughtn't to have*.

1 tell him that she had a new pet

She ought to have told him that she had a new pet.

2 ask him what he wanted for his birthday

3 arrive so early for the party

4 be late for the cinema

5 remember his passport

6 knock on the door before she entered

4 Vocabulary

Match these words with their definitions.

> available   consequence   consider
> essential   store   wipe out

1 result or effect
2 keep something to use later
3 destroy completely
4 absolutely necessary
5 think about
6 can be taken or used

5 Vocabulary

Match the verbs in list A with the words in list B. Then write the phrases.

	A	B	
1	build	electricity	1 *build a dam*
2	learn	a dam	2
3	generate	off a tap	3
4	displace	potatoes	4
5	produce	people	5
6	turn	lessons	6

6 Vocabulary

Match the words in list A with the words in list B and write six compound words.

	A	B	
1	under	can	1 *underway*
2	hose	cap	2
3	ice	way	3
4	rain	water	4
5	watering	pipe	5

7 Pronunciation

Write these words in the correct column.

> ~~amount~~ concern displace effect hygiene hosepipe
> litre major mistake polar shortage survive

▪■	■▪
amount	

> **Extension** Make a list of actions that could have prevented today's environmental problems.

8.2 NATURAL WORLD
What would you do?

1 Reading

Read the dialogue and complete the sentences on the right.

SAM Tim, what would you do if you were lost in a foreign country?
TIM I'd ask someone for help.
SAM Yes, but how could you ask for help if you didn't speak the language?
TIM Well, I'd try to find someone who could speak English.
SAM And what if you couldn't find an English speaker?
TIM I'd use a map.
SAM But what would you do if you didn't have a map?
TIM I'd phone you on my mobile and ask for help!

2 Second conditional

Write questions using the second conditional and answer them using phrases from the box.

call an ambulance   catch some fish   climb a tree
~~melt some snow~~   stay in bed

1 be in the Arctic and not have enough water

   What would you do if you were in the Arctic and didn't have enough water?
   I'd melt some snow.

2 be lost at sea and not have anything to eat

1 If Tim was lost in a foreign country,

2 If he didn't speak the language,

3 If he couldn't find someone who spoke English,

4 If he didn't have a map,

3 be in the jungle and meet a wild elephant

4 wake up at night and hear a noise

5 see an accident and have to get help

3 Second conditional

Write sentences using the second conditional.

1 I/be a millionaire/I/give all my money away
   If I were a millionaire, I'd give all my money away.

2 she/hurry/she/catch the train

3 he/ask me to go to the cinema/I/be delighted

4 they/work harder/they/finish the job today

5 you/not worry so much/you/be much happier

6 they/ask me/I/help them

4 Second conditional

Write sentences giving advice using these phrases.

> do as much as possible   ~~phone for a taxi~~   join a gym
> not buy so many clothes   send her some flowers
> ring and let her know

1 'I've just missed the last bus.'
   If I were you, I'd phone for a taxi.

2 'I never know what to wear.'

3 'It's her birthday today – what should I get her?'

4 'I want to take more exercise.'

5 'I can't do all this homework today.'

6 'I don't want to go to her party tonight.'

5 Vocabulary

Match these words with their definitions.

> crouch   dentist   join   magnifying glass
> oasis   object *n*   shelter   torch

1 when you look through it, things seem bigger

2 place with water in a desert

3 place where you are safe

4 thing

5 bend your knees so you are close to the ground

6 bring together

7 you carry it to see in the dark

8 person who looks after your teeth

6 Vocabulary

Find nine words or phrases to do with health and illness in the word square. Use the words to complete the sentences below.

H	I	C	C	O	U	G	H	S
E	H	U	B	A	E	J	T	O
A	S	P	I	R	I	N	O	R
D	E	N	T	I	S	T	O	E
A	T	W	R	L	H	A	T	T
C	O	U	G	H	G	N	H	H
H	M	V	I	D	L	U	A	R
E	D	O	C	T	O	R	C	O
E	T	C	O	L	D	P	H	A
S	N	B	R	I	G	K	E	T

1 If I hadn't cheered so loudly at the football match, I wouldn't have a _____ now.

2 Hold your breath to get rid of your _____.

3 Put your hand over your mouth when you _____.

4 You'll catch a _____! Put your coat on!

5 When my head hurts, I take an _____.

6 If you often get bad headaches, you should see a _____.

7 I'm going to see my _____ about this terrible _____.

7 Pronunciation

Do they rhyme (✔) or not (✘)?

1	honey	funny	✔
2	tight	bite	☐
3	breathe	breath	☐
4	cough	off	☐
5	hiccough	pick up	☐
6	spray	grey	☐
7	thread	bed	☐
8	join	one	☐
9	sore	saw	☐
10	torch	watch	☐

> **Extension** Ask a friend or a family member to do the *Survival Questionnaire* on page 102 of the Student's Book and justify their answers. Write a short paragraph explaining their answers. Use the second conditional!

UNIT 8

89

8.3 NATURAL WORLD
You'd like to stay there, wouldn't you?

1 Reading

Read Sophie and Zak's conversation and complete it with question tags.

ZAK Is that another photo from the unusual buildings website?

SOPHIE Yes, it is. You've seen some of these buildings before, (1) .... ?

ZAK Oh, I think I've seen a photo of that before. It's in Prague, (2) .... ?

SOPHIE Yes, that's right. It's called *The Dancing House*. It was designed by Frank Gehry.

ZAK He's an American, (3) .... ?

SOPHIE Yes, he's from California. The house really looks as if it is dancing, (4) .... ?

ZAK Yes it does. I think it's supposed to represent Fred Astaire and Ginger Rogers dancing.

SOPHIE They were famous American film stars, (5) .... ?

ZAK That's right.

SOPHIE You've never been to Prague on holiday, (6) .... ?

ZAK No, never. I'd love to go.

2 Question tags

Complete with these question tags.

| couldn't you did he did you didn't I didn't they hasn't it haven't we isn't it weren't they would they |

1 The buildings were all special in some way, ... ?

2 Zak didn't understand why they chose those particular buildings, ... ?

3 The Shanghai World Expo pavilion has been in the news recently, ... ?

4 You could make the building change colour by moving around in it, ... ?

5 After the Expo was over, they recycled the building, ... ?

6 The world's biggest igloo is in Canada, ... ?

7 You didn't know that the world's tallest skyscraper was in Dubai, ... ?

8 They wouldn't let Zak into the world's most expensive hotel, ... ?

9 We've seen that picture before, ... ?

10 I asked you to bring the camera, ... ?

3 Question tags

Complete with question tags.

1 *The Call of the Wild* is about a dog called Buck, ... ?

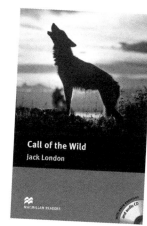

2 Jack London couldn't find any gold in the Yukon, ... ?

3 He made a lot of money from his books, ... ?

4 People in the Yukon needed dogs to help them carry things, ... ?

5 In winter the rivers in the Yukon freeze, ... ?

6 Buck's owner is called John Thornton, ... ?

7 Thornton's dogs were like children to him, ... ?

8 Books about looking for gold are exciting, ... ?

4 Question tags

Complete with question tags.

1 Bethany was surfing with her best friend Alana, ... ?

2 She wanted to become a professional surfer, ... ?

3 The sea wasn't at all rough, ... ?

4 The girls were waiting for the next big wave, ... ?

5 Bethany couldn't do anything when the shark attacked, ... ?

6 She didn't scream, ... ?

7 She knew she had to get back to the beach quickly, ... ?

8 At first she couldn't feel any pain, ... ?

9 She has won surf competitions, ... ?

10 They made a film about her called *Soul Surfer*, ... ?

5 Vocabulary

Match the verbs in list A with the words in list B.

	A	B
1	expect	colour
2	let	something out of something
3	be	a motorbike
4	win	someone in
5	ride	someone to know something
6	make	in the news
7	change	a medal

6 Crossword

Complete the crossword and find this word ↓.

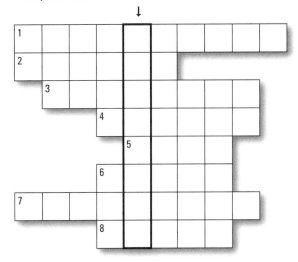

1 The pavilion in Shanghai was built for an … .
2 The pavilion changed … when people moved inside it.
3 Frank Gehry … *The Dancing House*.
4 The Dubai skyscraper has got 160 of these.
5 The house on the roof of the art museum is upside … .
6 It costs £4,500 a … to stay in the Governor Villa.
7 The Governor Villa is one of the world's most … hotel suites.
8 This building is made of ice and it's called an … .

7 Pronunciation

Mark the stressed syllable.

■
exhibition   expensive   igloo   pavilion   skyscraper
unusual

> **Extension** Write a paragraph about your favourite building or an unusual building you know.

8.4 NATURAL WORLD

Integrated Skills
Describing a country

1 Reading

Read and complete the description of New Zealand with these phrases.

a the name means *normal* or *ordinary* in the Maori language
b but has more volcanoes
c and the film and wine industries are developing
d and in 1840 Britain made it a colony
e and 80% of its plants are only found there
f while Auckland receives three times that amount
g 2,000 kilometres south-east of Australia
h full of large birds which could not fly
i on the South Island

NEW ZEALAND

New Zealand is made up of two large islands and many small ones. Its total area is 268,680 square km, making it the 73rd largest country in the world. It lies in the south-western Pacific Ocean, (**1**) _____. The population of New Zealand is about 4.4 million and the capital city is Wellington, on the North Island. The official languages are English and Maori.

The people
No one lived in New Zealand until 600–800 years ago. Then people arrived by boat from Polynesia and founded the Maori culture. A Dutch sailor, Abel Janszoon Tasman, was the first European to discover New Zealand in 1642. European sailors who were hunting whales started to visit the islands, (**2**) _____. New Zealand became independent in 1907. The Maori people – (**3**) _____ – make up about 15% of the population. Auckland is the largest city with a population of 1,355,000.

Geography
The South Island is the larger of the two main islands. The highest mountain is Aoraki (Mount Cook) at 3,754 metres and there are 18 more mountains over 3,000 metres (**4**) _____. The North Island has fewer mountains (**5**) _____. The dramatic New Zealand countryside has attracted many TV and film crews.

Wildlife
New Zealand has always been far from the rest of the world, so animals and plants have developed differently (**6**) _____. Until the arrival of humans, the islands were covered in forests, (**7**) _____. Unfortunately, most of these were soon killed.

Industry and agriculture
Major industries include agriculture, fishing, forestry and information technology. Tourism is important, (**8**) _____.

Weather
New Zealand's typical climate is cool to warm. Average temperatures usually never go below 0˚C or rise above 30˚C. The driest city is Christchurch, which gets only 640mm of rain a year, (**9**) _____.

2 Read the sentences and write *T* (true) or *F* (false).

1 The population of Auckland is 4,000,000. ☐
2 The Maoris came from Europe. ☐
3 85% of the population are not Maori. ☐
4 There are more volcanoes on the North Island. ☐
5 80% of the plants can be found in the rest of the world. ☐
6 Christchurch is three times as dry as Auckland. ☐

UNIT 8

3 Use these notes to write a similar text about South Africa.

SOUTH AFRICA
In southern part of African continent. Area 1,219,912 square km. 24th largest country. Atlantic Ocean to west, Indian Ocean to east. Population 49,320,000. Three capital cities: Cape Town, Pretoria, Bloemfontein. 11 official languages.

The people
People have lived in South Africa longer than almost anywhere else. Dutch sailor, Jan van Riebeeck, one of first Europeans to live there in 1652. 1805 Britain made part of it a colony. Became independent 1961. Johannesburg largest city, population 3,890,000.

Geography
Wide variety of countryside from desert to subtropical. Grassland and mountains in interior. Coast 2,500 km long.

Wildlife
20,000 different plants but few forests. Lions, leopards, elephants, giraffes and other animals in National Parks.

Industry and agriculture
Major: gold and diamond mining. Tourism and wine production developing.

Weather
Wide variety of temperature. Lowest −15°C in mountains. Highest 51.7°C in desert in 1948.

4 Crossword

Complete the crossword.

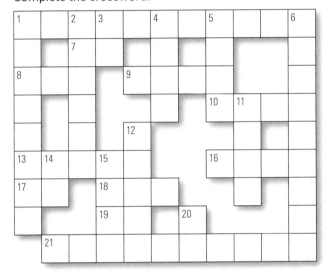

Across →
1. The average ... in Sydney in July is 8°C to 16°C. (11)
7. Contraction of *I am*. (2)
8. Plural of *my*. (3)
9. Opposite of *there*. (4)
10. It's between your eyes. (4)
13, 4 Down   The Great Barrier is a ... (5, 4)
16. Opposite of *east*. (4)
17. Australia is ... island. (2)
18. Australia has a ... of sunshine. (3)
19. Why are you ... concerned about water? (2)
21. The Australian government is trying to preserve the ... culture. (10)

Down ↓
1. There are ... rainforests in the north of Australia. (8)
2. You can see yourself in a ... (6)
3. Afternoon or evening. (2)
4. See 13 Across. (4)
5. Aborigines lived in Australia for 50,000 years, but ... Europeans came. (4)
6. Something which you can't live without is ... (9)
11. Opposite of *closed*. (4)
12. You walk on this inside a building. (5)
14. Sydney is ... the south-east coast of Australia. (2)
15. There are hurricanes and cyclones, but droughts are ... common. (4)
20. Short for *for example*. (2)

LEARNER INDEPENDENCE

English club
Start an English club with a group of friends. Meet regularly, perhaps once a week, and do things together in English. Activities might include discussing a film, having a tea party with an English-speaking guest or organising a quiz night.

Extensive reading
Read *Meet Me in Istanbul* and write a new ending for the story.

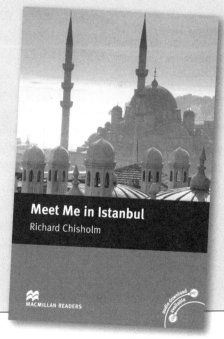

Tom Smith flies to Turkey to join his fiancée, Angela, for a holiday in Istanbul. But Angela fails to meet him that evening as arranged. The next morning Tom has some terrible news; Angela was killed in a driving accident – a week ago!

8 NATURAL WORLD
Inspiration EXTRA!

REVISION

LESSON 1

Complete with *should have* or *shouldn't have* and these verbs.

> be buy feed forget ~~remember~~ reply turn write

1 You *should have remembered* to lock the door.
2 You _____ more polite to the teacher.
3 She _____ to post the letter.
4 He _____ a present for his mother.
5 They _____ the animals at the zoo.
6 I _____ off the computer. I want to use it.
7 You _____ to their invitation. Now it's too late.
8 He _____ a thank-you letter after the visit.

LESSON 2

Write sentences using the second conditional.

1 you/listen carefully/you/not get things wrong
   If you listened carefully, you wouldn't get things wrong.
2 she/ask me/I/ be delighted to help
3 the band/practise more/they/play much better
4 you/give me your box of matches/I/light a fire
5 I/have enough money/I/get some new trainers
6 it/snow/we/go skiing tomorrow
7 I/win the lottery/I/travel to New Zealand
8 what/you/do/you/see a bear

LESSON 3

Complete with question tags.

1 It's time to go, *isn't it* ?
2 It wasn't a good film, _____ ?
3 You'd like to visit Dubai, _____ ?
4 They didn't want to stay in the igloo, _____ ?
5 Leonardo da Vinci invented the first car, _____ ?
6 Paper was invented in China, _____ ?
7 Kate Winslet wasn't in *Avatar*, _____ ?
8 He thought the film was boring, _____ ?

LESSON 4

Match these words with their definitions.

1 coastal ☐
2 currency ☐
3 drought ☐
4 hurricane ☐
5 interior ☐
6 plain *n* ☐
7 temperature ☐
8 tropical ☐

a how hot or cold something is
b money used in a particular country
c very strong storm with wind and rain
d there are monsoons in or from the hottest parts of the world
e by the sea
f large flat area
g when there is no rain for a long time
h inner part of a country, far away from the sea

Spelling

Correct the spelling of these words from Unit 8. One letter is wrong in each word.

1 availible   2 commen   3 considaribly   4 essentiel
5 extrimely   6 hiccouphs   7 interier   8 mountein
9 priserve   10 shalter   11 shortige   12 tipical

Brainteaser

Luke has it first and Paul has it last. Millions have it twice but thousands don't have it at all.

Answer on page 97.

UNIT 8

EXTENSION

LESSON 1

Write three sentences using *should have* or *shouldn't have* about yourself, and three about a friend.

1 *I shouldn't have got angry with my parents.*
2
3
4
5
6
7

LESSON 2

Write sentences about yourself.

If you were a(n) …, what … would you be? Why?

1 animal
   If I were an animal, I'd be a shark because they're so powerful.
2 kind of weather
3 item of clothing
4 island
5 film
6 drink
7 sport
8 picture
9 cartoon character
10 building

LESSON 3

Write sentences with question tags about people in *New Inspiration 3*.

1 Tony *is the director of Star School, isn't he?*
2 Ron Hornbaker
3 Richard Smith and Luke Bateman
4 Maurice Grosse
5 Ewan McGregor
6 Benjamin Zephaniah
7 Louis Braille
8 Ray Tomlinson

LESSON 4

Write a short paragraph in your notebook about an imaginary country OR about a country which you didn't describe in exercise 6 on page 107 of the Student's Book.

Web watch

Simple English Wikipedia is a free online encyclopedia written in simple English. Anyone can write or edit entries. Look up your town or country. Read what it says and correct the entry if necessary. If there isn't an entry for your town or country, you might like to add one.

Spelling

Read and complete the words.

The sound /əl/ at the end of a word is usually spelt *-al*, *-el* or *-le*.

1 Aborigin____ 2 availab____ 3 cand____ 4 coast____
5 considerab____ 6 continent____ 7 environment____
8 essenti____ 9 jung____ 10 need____ 11 nov____ 12 offici____
13 trav____ 14 tropic____ 15 typic____ 16 vehic____

Brainteaser

What travels around the world but always stays in a corner?

Answer on page 97.

1 Read and complete. For each number 1–12, choose

95

REVIEW
UNITS 7–8

word or phrase A, B, C or D.

SNOWBOARDERS MOUNTAIN RESCUE

How (1) _____ you survive if you were lost on a mountain in the snow? Amazingly, two snowboarders were found alive after nearly three days in temperatures of –15°C, and one of them had a broken leg.

Jessica Townsend (17) and Pete Baxter (16) were on a snowboarding holiday with a school group, when they got lost in the Swiss Alps near the resort of Champéry. Their teachers immediately reported that Jessica and Pete (2) _____, but it took rescue services over 60 hours to find them. The teenagers were finally picked up by helicopter and are now recovering in hospital.

'We (3) _____ left the group,' said Jessica, 'but we didn't understand how easy it was to get lost. And then it got dark. That was when things really went wrong – Pete fell badly and hit a tree. Then he told me he (4) _____ his leg.'

Pete continued the story. 'I didn't scream, (5) _____? But the pain was terrible. I tried to get up, but Jessica told me (6) _____.'

She made a kind of shelter with our snowboards, but it was still freezing cold. And we got very hungry, because we only had a couple of sandwiches and some chocolate in our daypacks.'

The teenagers guessed that people were looking for them, because they kept hearing the sound of a helicopter. Finally, Jessica climbed up above the tree line, and waved her yellow anorak until the rescue helicopter saw her.

The paramedics asked the teenagers (7) _____ they hadn't got mobile phones. Jessica replied that she had a mobile in her pocket, but the battery was flat. 'I (8) _____ checked that my phone was turned off, but I didn't realise until it was too late,' she said. Pete explained that he (9) _____ his phone when he fell. 'I know I (10) _____ be alive if it weren't for Jessica,' he added.

'We're both lucky to be alive, (11) _____?' said Jessica. The teenagers promised they (12) _____ never leave the group again.

1	A do	B did	C will	D would
2	A are missing	B were missing	C missed	D had missed
3	A should	B shouldn't	C should have	D shouldn't have
4	A has broken	B broke	C had broken	D was broken
5	A did I	B didn't I	C was I	D wasn't I
6	A not moving	B not move	C not to move	D not moved
7	A why	B where	C when	D that
8	A should	B shouldn't	C should have	D shouldn't have
9	A has lost	B did lose	C was lost	D had lost
10	A can't	B won't	C didn't	D wouldn't
11	A are we	B aren't we	C isn't it	D aren't they
12	A will	B won't	C would	D wouldn't

2 Complete with the correct form of the words in capitals.

1 After a hot dry summer, there was a water _____. SHORT

2 I got your email but I can't open the _____. ATTACH

3 _____ is an important industry for many countries. TOUR

4 She waved to attract the _____ of the waiter. ATTEND

5 Tourists should be careful not to cause _____ damage. ENVIRONMENT

6 Don't eat those mushrooms – they could be _____! POISON

7 Huge waves damaged buildings in _____ towns. COAST

8 _____ glasses aren't as powerful as microscopes. MAGNIFY

96

3 Complete the second sentence so that it means the same as the first sentence.

1 'Can everyone smile, please?' said the photographer.
   The photographer asked everyone _____

2 'I can't remember,' Ray said to the interviewer.
   Ray told the interviewer that _____

3 'Bethany, how long have you been a surfer?' the reporter asked.
   The reporter asked Bethany _____

4 'What's the weather like in Australia?' Anna asked.
   Anna asked what _____

5 Why didn't you ask me for help?
   You should _____

6 They were silly to miss the last bus.
   They shouldn't _____

7 She lost her bag, but she didn't go to the police station!
   If I _____

8 I think you should go to the dentist.
   If I _____

4 Find the odd word.

1 dentist   doctor   hospital   nurse
2 cold   cough   headache   illness
3 cause   consequence   effect   result
4 ambulance   coastguard   emergency   police
5 ask   answer   reply   respond
6 amazing   average   extraordinary   phenomenal
7 boat   dinghy   lake   ship
8 emu   koala   ape   zebra
9 candle   match   torch   whistle
10 climate   cyclone   hurricane   monsoon

Answers to Brainteasers

UNIT 7	UNIT 8
Revision a promise	**Revision** the letter L
Extension nothing	**Extension** a stamp on a letter

LEARNER INDEPENDENCE
SELF ASSESSMENT

Vocabulary

1 Draw this chart in your notebook. How many words can you write in each category?

More than 10? Good!   *More than 12?* Very good!
More than 15? Excellent!

Internet	
Environment	
Illnesses and Ailments	

2 Put the words in order to make expressions from the phrasebooks in Lesson 4 in Units 7 and 8.

1 exactly remember can't I
   I can't remember exactly.

2 answer easy isn't there an
   _____

3 did how get idea you the
   _____

4 headache a I've got
   _____

5 a problem it's tough
   _____

6 joking must you be
   _____

7 do what you would
   _____

8 were I if you I'd
   _____

Check your answers.
8/8 Excellent!   6/8 Very good!   4/8 Try again!

My learning diary
In Units 7 and 8:
My favourite topic is _____

My favourite picture is _____

The three lessons I like most are _____

My favourite activity or exercise is _____

97

L.A. BLUES

1 Someone was in my office

 Look at the picture. Who are the people? What is the woman saying to the man?

I work in Los Angeles. My office is on West 14th Street in Hollywood. There's a glass door with my name on it: *Lenny Samuel – Private Detective*.

It was a Monday morning in July. I was in my office with my feet on the desk. The phone wasn't ringing. I didn't have any visitors. And I didn't have any money. I needed money to pay for my new car, a midnight blue Chevrolet. So I was unhappy. I had the blues – the L.A. blues.

I looked at my watch. Ten o'clock. Time for coffee in Al's Diner. I was wearing a dark blue suit, a smart red tie, and a light blue shirt. Yes, blue's my favorite colour. My eyes are blue, too.

After I finished my coffee, I walked back to my office. But I stopped outside and looked through the glass door. Someone was in my office. The visitor was holding something – it looked like a gun. I kicked the door open and pushed the visitor across the office. We both fell onto the floor.

'Are you Mr Samuel?' the visitor asked. 'Do you always welcome people like this?'

It was a woman! In her hand she held a phone – not a gun! She stood up quickly and looked down at me. She was wearing a smart jacket and trousers. She had curly red hair and green eyes. She looked about 25. She also looked like a million dollars.

'I'm sorry,' I said. 'I thought you had a gun.'

The woman smiled. 'Get up. I have a job for you.'

I sat down at my desk.

'Please sit down,' I said very politely.

'I prefer to stand,' said the woman. 'About this job – how much do you charge?'

'$500 a day,' I replied.

'All right,' she said. 'I want you to find someone. His name is Mark Jackson, and he works for Metro Rent-A-Car on Los Feliz Boulevard. He disappeared a week ago.'

She gave me Mark Jackson's photograph and his home address.

'What's your name and address?' I asked.

'Just call me Ann. You don't need my address,' she answered. 'See you here at ten tomorrow morning. Goodbye, Mr Samuel.'

Ann smiled again and walked out of the office.

 Why do you think Ann is looking for Mark Jackson?

L.A. BLUES

2 Where was El Mayor?

 Look at the picture. Where is Lenny? What do you think he is asking?

I looked at the photo of Mark Jackson. He was about 25, with long brown hair. He had a big nose and a big smile.

I left the office and drove to Los Feliz Boulevard. I parked the Chevrolet outside the Metro Rent-A-Car office and went in. A young blonde woman in a red suit smiled at me. A badge on her suit said 'Hi, I'm Julie.'

'Good morning, sir. Can I help you?' she asked.

'I'm trying to find Mark Jackson,' I replied.

Julie looked at me in a strange way. 'You can ask Mr Vargas, but he's busy right now.'

'I can wait,' I replied. A few minutes later, a man came out of Vargas's office. He was wearing sunglasses, a leather jacket, and very expensive cowboy boots. He walked straight past Julie and out to the street.

I went into the office. Vargas was a short, fat man in his fifties with a red face.

'I'm looking for Mark Jackson,' I said.

'There's no one here named Mark Jackson,' Vargas said. His face got redder.

'I see,' I said slowly and walked out of his office.

'Thanks for your help,' I said to Julie. I waved goodbye and left.

I drove to Mark Jackson's apartment on Emerson Avenue. Apartment 132 was on the first floor. I rang the bell. No reply. I know how to open doors, and a minute later I was inside the apartment.

In Jackson's living room, there was a stereo, and there were lots of CDs. I turned on the stereo and a favourite song of mine started playing – *Goodbye Summer Blues*. I searched the living room. Then I went into the bedroom. I checked the jackets and trousers in the wardrobe. There was a piece of paper in one of the pockets that said: 'Casa Dorada, El Mayor.'

Where was El Mayor?

Then I heard a man's voice behind me.

'Who are you?' he asked and pushed something hard into my back. It felt like a gun. I looked in the mirror in front of me. I could only see part of the man behind me. He was wearing a leather jacket.

'Are you a police officer?' I asked him.

'I'm asking the questions!' he replied. 'Who are you?'

I looked in the mirror again. This time I could see the gun in the man's hand. It was above my head. Just before I hit the floor, I saw a pair of very expensive cowboy boots. That was the last thing I remembered.

 What happened to Lenny? Who is the man with the gun?

L.A. BLUES

3 You'd better get someone else

 Look at the picture. How does Lenny feel? What is he pointing to?

When I opened my eyes, I was still in Mark Jackson's apartment. But now all the books, CDs, and clothes were on the floor. And my head hurt.

'What was Cowboy Boots looking for?' I asked myself.

But I couldn't think properly, and I was very tired. I drove home to my apartment in Santa Monica and went to bed. I woke up at 9.30 the next morning.

'Oh, no – I'm going to be late,' I thought. 'Ann won't be pleased.'

When I arrived at my office, Ann was sitting at my desk.

'You're late, Mr Samuel,' Ann said. 'I got here over half an hour ago.'

I looked at Ann and laughed.

'It isn't funny,' she said.

'No, it isn't,' I agreed. 'Look at my head.' Ann looked worried. 'What happened?' she asked.

I told her about my visit to Metro Rent-A-Car. I told her about Mark Jackson's apartment and the man in the cowboy boots.

'I've had enough. You'd better get someone else to find Mark Jackson.'

Ann looked at me for a moment. Then she stood up and put her hand on my arm.

'I'm sorry, Mr Samuel,' she said slowly. 'There's something I didn't tell you.'

'I think there's a lot you didn't tell me. I don't even know your last name.'

'My last name is Jackson,' she said slowly. 'I'm Mark's sister. I'm from Dallas, Texas.'

I looked at her, but I didn't say anything. Why didn't she have a Texas accent?

'Mark called me last Monday,' she went on. 'He was somewhere in Mexico, and he was there to pick up a Metro car. He should be back in L.A. now. But he isn't …'

'Why didn't you tell me this yesterday?' I asked.

'Because private detectives like you don't want trouble. And I think Mark is in real danger.'

I stood there, thinking. I didn't really believe her. But I knew one thing – I wanted to see her again.

'OK,' I said at last. 'I'll look for Mark in Mexico.'

'And I'm coming with you.'

'All right, you can come. But you don't have to call me Mr Samuel. You can call me Lenny.'

She smiled. 'Meet me at the Roosevelt Hotel in three hours, Lenny.'

After Ann left, I sat and thought.

'Time to pay another visit to Metro Rent-A-Car,' I decided.

When I got there, Julie smiled nervously and looked quickly around the office. We were alone.

'Mr Vargas told me not to say anything,' she said quietly. 'But Mark *did* work here.'

'Why did Vargas lie about that?' I asked.

'I don't know, but there was a phone call on Monday that scared him,' Julie replied.

'One last question. Where did Mark go in Mexico?' I asked. 'Was it a place called El Mayor?'

Julie didn't answer, but the look on her face told me I was right.

 What happens when Lenny and Ann go to Mexico?

L.A. BLUES

4 I heard someone coming

 Look at the picture. Where are Lenny and Ann? Who are they talking to?

I drove back to my apartment, got some clothes, and then went to the Roosevelt Hotel.

Ann was waiting outside. She was wearing jeans and a purple shirt. I put her bag in the back of the Chevrolet.

'Let's go to Mexico!' she said.

Then she sat back and closed her eyes. I drove on, with the blue Pacific on our right. We passed San Diego and crossed the border at Tijuana. An hour later, I turned inland, and finally we arrived in a small town. Ann opened her eyes.

'Where are we?' she asked.

'El Mayor. Now we're going to find the Casa Dorada,' I said.

It was getting late, and we were getting hungry. We went into a small café and ordered some enchiladas. I asked the waiter in Spanish how to get to the Casa Dorada.

'It's at the end of that road,' he answered in English, and pointed.

We left the café and drove in the dark until we came to some woods by a lake. The Casa Dorada was an old wooden house near the water. There were some small cabins behind it, but they were all dark. I parked in front of a sign that said: *Casa Dorada – Cabins to Rent*.

The entrance hall was empty. I rang the bell on the desk. Nothing happened. Ann opened a large book on the desk – it contained the names of guests at the Casa Dorada. We looked through the book. Then we noticed a page was missing.

'The page for last week – that's when Mark stayed in El Mayor!' Ann said.

Then I heard someone coming. 'Can I help you?' a voice said.

A thin, dark-haired man in his late thirties stood at the door. He didn't smile.

'I'm Hank. I'm the manager.'

'We'd like two cabins for the night,' I said.

'Sorry. We're full.' Hank walked to the desk and closed the large book with a bang.

'Perhaps this will help.' I gave Hank 25 dollars.

'OK,' he said. 'I just remembered. There's one empty cabin – cabin 13. It's $100 a night. You pay now.'

Cabin 13 had a kitchen, bathroom, living room and bedroom.

'I'll sleep in the cabin,' said Ann. 'You can sleep in the car.'

She opened the door. I smiled and walked out. I never argue with women.

I made myself comfortable on the back seat of the Chevrolet, and I soon fell asleep.

A noise woke me at sunrise. I heard a plane flying over the lake. It was a yellow seaplane. It flew low over the middle of the lake and then flew away to the west. I looked back at the lake. There was a small red flag floating in the middle. Then I heard a small boat crossing the lake. It was going towards the small red flag. The boat stopped for a minute by the flag and then came back to the shore. The man in the boat was Hank.

He was carrying a small metal box, which he took into the Casa Dorada.

 What is in the metal box?

L.A. BLUES

5 Where have you been?

Look at the picture. Where is Ann? What is she doing?

I went to cabin 13 and knocked. There was no answer, so I opened the door and went in. Ann's bag was on the floor, but she wasn't there.

I was beginning to get worried, when Ann came back.

'Where have you been?' I asked. 'I have something to tell you.'

'Let me guess,' said Ann. 'You saw a plane flying over the lake, and it dropped something into the water. Hank went out in a boat to get it.'

I looked at her in surprise.

'I've taken some pictures,' Ann explained, holding up her camera. 'Are you a good swimmer?'

'Not bad. Why?'

'I want to swim out to that flag. And I don't want Hank to see us. Let's do it now.'

A few minutes later, we were in the lake. Ann was wearing a blue swimsuit. She started swimming underwater. I followed her. We swam for as long as we could and then came up for air. We breathed deeply and then went under again.

The flag was tied to the bottom of the lake by a rope. We dived down, following the rope. The water was dark. Then Ann pointed at something. It was a man's body. There were heavy weights around his feet. It was a man of about 50.

And it definitely wasn't Mark Jackson.

When we got back to the cabin, we were silent for a few minutes.

'Who can the man in the lake be?' I asked.

'I've no idea,' she answered. 'At least it's not Mark. But I'm sure Mark was here last week.' She looked at me. 'So what do we do now?'

I shook my head. I sat down on the bed and stared at the floor. Then I noticed something – a small piece of yellow paper under the bed. I pulled it out. It was a ticket. On one side, it said: Ensenada Seaplane Tours. On the other side, there was one word in handwriting – *Coromandel*. I showed the ticket to Ann.

'That's Mark's writing! He *has* been here! Ensenada is a town on the coast. Perhaps he's there now,' she said.

'There's only one way to find out,' I replied.

When we reached Ensenada, I stopped and asked the way to *Ensenada Seaplane Tours*.

We drove on to the place where the seaplane tours started. I sat in a café while Ann went off for a ride in the plane.

When she came back, she looked excited.

'It's the same seaplane we saw this morning. We flew over a ship out at sea,' she said. 'I've taken some photos of it. And I could see its name – *Coromandel*!'

What are Lenny and Ann going to do next?

L.A. BLUES

6 It contained thousands of dollars!

Look at the picture. Who are the people? What is happening?

We watched the seaplane all afternoon. It made nine trips around the harbour with five or six passengers each time. But the tenth trip was different. This time, there were only two passengers. One was a well-dressed man of about 50, with white hair. The second was Hank. The plane took off and flew straight out to sea.

I turned to Ann. 'It's landing by the *Coromandel*. We have to get closer to the ship.'

We rented a small motorboat. I started the engine and pointed the boat out to sea. It had become dark, but we could see the lights of a ship ahead of us.

I turned off the engine. There was a ladder down the side of the ship. When I had tied the motorboat to the ladder, Ann and I climbed onto the ship. We moved silently toward the lights at the back of the ship. Then we looked down.

Three men were sitting around a table. One of the men was Hank. The man next to him was wearing a cap and was probably the ship's captain.

The third man had white hair. I'd seen him with Hank earlier. He had a metal box in front of him, and a notebook was open beside it.

Ann took pictures. No one looked up at us. They were watching the white-haired man. He opened the box and took out a package. He gave it to the captain, who opened it. It contained thousands of dollars! After the captain had counted the money carefully, he gave the white-haired man a little bag.

The white-haired man emptied the bag onto the table. It contained small bright stones. He looked at them carefully and touched them gently. I remembered reading that real diamonds always feel cold. Then he put one finger in his mouth and touched some of the stones with it. The stones stayed on his finger. False diamonds don't do that.

Ann took some more pictures. At that moment, Hank looked up and saw us.

'Dr Summers – look!' he shouted to the white-haired man. I took Ann's hand and we ran back to the other end of the ship.

'There's only one way we can get to the motorboat now. Come on!' Ann shouted.

How can Lenny and Ann escape?

L.A. BLUES

7 The driver had an accident

 Look at the picture. Who are the people? What is happening?

Ann and I dived into the water and swam to the motorboat. I turned on the engine and pointed the boat back towards the shore. There were some shots fired from the ship, but we were already too far away.

'It's time to go back to L.A. We're not welcome here anymore,' I said.

Ann drove, and I fell asleep beside her. When I woke up, it was morning, and we were in L.A. Ann said she was tired and needed some sleep.

'OK. I'll call you later,' I said.

Then I drove to the Metro Rent-A-Car office.

'Hi,' Julie said when she saw me. 'How are you?'

'Fine, thanks,' I replied. 'Tell me, does the name Dr Summers mean anything to you?'

Julie replied that Dr Summers' clinic had rented lots of cars from them. 'Usually a driver from the clinic takes the car to Mexico and brings a patient back to L.A. But last time, the driver had an accident.'

I asked what kind of accident it had been.

'I don't know – but Mark was sent to Mexico to drive the car back.' Julie was getting nervous.

'Did you see the driver from the clinic?' I asked. Then I described the man in the lake.

'Yes, that's what the driver looked like,' Julie said. Suddenly, Vargas opened his office door.

'Julie!' he shouted. 'Walter will kill us both if he finds out we've talked to anyone!'

I knew who Walter was. He was the man with the sunglasses, the leather jacket, and the cowboy boots.

'You won't be killed, Mr Vargas. Because you aren't going to tell Walter that I've been here!' I said.

Before I left, I asked Julie if Mark had a Texas accent.

'Yes,' she said.

Back in my apartment, I looked up Dr Summers in the phone book and I found the address of his clinic – the Summerview Clinic.

I sat there thinking. If Ann was from Texas, why didn't she have a Texas accent? Was she really Mark Jackson's sister? If she wasn't, why was she looking for him? I liked Ann, but I didn't believe her story.

The next morning, I drove to the Summerview Clinic. I parked behind an ambulance and got out of the car.

Suddenly, a white Cadillac drove up and a man got out. He was wearing sunglasses, a leather jacket, and cowboy boots – Walter. Walter disappeared into the clinic. A few minutes later, he came out with a white-haired man – Dr Summers. They were carrying another man between them.

He was about 25, with long brown hair and a big nose. But he wasn't smiling.

 Who is the man with long brown hair?

L.A. BLUES

8 I should have guessed!

Look at the picture. What is Ann showing Lenny?

I recognized the man from his photograph. It was Mark Jackson.

'Where did you hide the diamonds?' I heard Summers ask.

Jackson didn't – or couldn't – reply.

'OK, we're going back to the Casa Dorada. Then you can show us where the diamonds are.'

Summers and Walter threw Jackson into the back of the Cadillac. Then they got in the front of the car and drove off.

I ran back to the Chevrolet and called Ann.

'They've got Mark!' I said when she answered. I told her quickly what I'd seen and heard.

'Be outside the hotel in half an hour,' I told her. 'We're going back to El Mayor.'

On my way to the Roosevelt Hotel, I remembered something. The CD on the stereo in Jackson's apartment was playing *Goodbye Summer Blues*. Perhaps the song was a clue. 'Summer' could mean Dr Summers. But what did 'blues' mean?

When I reached the Roosevelt, Ann jumped into the car. She looked pleased.

'Hi, Lenny! I have something to show you.'

They were the photos she had taken in Mexico: Hank taking the box from the lake, Dr Summers giving money to the ship's captain, Dr Summers looking at the diamonds.

One of the photos showed the open notebook I'd seen on the table beside the metal box. There was a list of colors:

Blue, Blue-white, Finest white, White, Silver, Finest light brown.

Next to the colors were numbers and dates. Then I saw the word 'carats' and I understood. 'Carats' is the word that describes the quality of diamonds. The colors were different kinds of diamonds, and the numbers were the value of the diamonds in carats.

'You're a very good photographer.' Then I added, 'But you aren't a very good liar, are you?'

'What do you mean?' Ann asked angrily.

'What's your real name? You aren't Mark's sister, are you?'

She looked at me. 'No, my real name is Ann Rivers.'

'If you told me the truth, I'd be able to help you more,' I said. 'Who are you working for?'

'I can't tell you yet. Trust me,' Ann replied.

I shook my head.

As we drove to El Mayor, the song *Goodbye Summer Blues* came back into my head. Then I remembered the list in Dr Summers's notebook – 'blues' were a kind of diamond! I should have guessed! Summers bought the diamonds on the ship, and then the seaplane flew them to the Casa Dorada. But how had Mark got the diamonds? And why had he hidden them?

L.A. BLUES

We stopped about a kilometre from the Casa Dorada, and we walked toward the house. The white Cadillac was outside. Suddenly, Summers, Hank and Walter came out.

'Quick,' Ann whispered. She took out her phone and ran towards the lake.

I tried to follow her, but I was too slow. Walter reached me first. 'You again!' he shouted. 'Let me kill him!'

'Wait!' Summers shouted. 'Who is he? How did he get here? Is he alone?'

Then Walter pointed to the lake. 'Look! There's a woman in the water! I'll get her!'

Summers ordered Hank to take me to the house. Hank pulled me into a small room. A man with long brown hair was lying on the floor. Hank left, locking the door.

'Hi, I'm Lenny Samuel, private detective,' I said. 'And you're Mark Jackson. Now tell me what's going on.'

◆ **What do you think is going on? What is going to happen?**

9 The L.A. blues had gone!

◆ **Look at the picture. What are Lenny and Mark talking about?**

'OK. I work for the US Customs,' Jackson explained. 'We believed Summers was smuggling diamonds from Mexico into the States in cars from Metro Rent-A-Car. That's why I got a job at Metro – to check all the cars that Summers used. Then Summers' driver was killed.'

'You mean the man in the lake?'

'Yes. He was killed because he tried to tell the police about Summers,' Jackson explained.

'So you came here to pick up the Metro car,' I said.

'Yes. I stayed the night at the Casa Dorada. While Hank was asleep, I searched the car. I found the diamonds and hid them. I planned to drive back to L.A., and then tell my people and the Mexican police where the diamonds were.'

'What went wrong?' I asked.

'When I stopped at the border, Walter was waiting with a gun. He searched the car. He discovered that the diamonds were missing and took me to the clinic. You know the rest.'

L.A. BLUES

'I don't know where you hid the diamonds,' I said.

Then the door opened. Ann was standing there, with Summers and Walter behind her. Summers was holding a gun to Ann's head.

'Jackson – for the last time, where are the diamonds?' Summers demanded. 'Tell me, or I shoot the woman!'

'OK, OK,' replied Jackson. 'The diamonds are at the bottom of the lake, under the flag.'

'Thank you, Mr Jackson,' smiled Summers. 'Come on, Samuel.'

They took me and Ann out of the house. Hank pulled Ann over to the lake and into the boat. He took the boat into the middle of the lake, stopped by the flag, and Ann dived in. Finally, she came up with a box in her hands. The boat came back to the shore.

'Give me the box,' Summers ordered. He opened it and smiled. 'My diamonds!'

He nodded to Walter and Hank. 'Take Samuel and the girl for a walk. We don't need them now.'

Walter and Hank marched me and Ann towards the trees. I felt Walter's gun in my back. I closed my eyes. There were two shots.

I opened my eyes and turned round. Ann was OK. Hank was on the ground, and he was dead.

Walter had dropped his gun, and his hands were in the air. Three men stepped out of the woods. Two were police officers with guns. They were holding Summers.

'Mr Samuel?' the third man asked. He had a neat moustache. 'I'm Captain Jimenez of the Mexican police. Pleased to meet you.'

'And I'm pleased to see *you*,' I replied. 'But how did you know we were here?'

Captain Jimenez turned to Ann. 'This young lady is from the US Customs, and she called us on her phone. The Mexican police work closely with US Customs. And now we have proof that Summers is a smuggler and a murderer.'

I looked at Ann. 'You're full of surprises,' I said.

Ann smiled. 'I'm sorry, Lenny, I haven't been completely honest with you. Don't be angry.'

'But I was attacked and nearly killed!' I cried. 'And I never know if you're telling the truth!'

'But I'm telling the truth now. I think you're wonderful.' She walked up and kissed me.

Then we walked to the lake. It was still summer. And the L.A. blues had gone!

 What do you think Lenny's next job will be?

107

L.A. BLUES

1 Someone was in my office

1 Answer the questions.

1. What is Lenny Samuel's job?
2. Why did he need money?
3. What did he do at ten o'clock?
4. Why did he push his visitor across the office?
5. What did Ann want Lenny to do?

2 Write words from page 98.

five words for clothes
suit,

five words for colours
midnight blue,

four words for parts of the body
feet,

3 Write sentences describing the picture on page 98.

2 Where was El Mayor?

1 Look at these sentences from the story. Who or what do the words in bold refer to?

1. **He** had a big nose and a big smile.
2. 'Good morning, **sir**.'
3. 'Can I help you?' **she** asked.
4. **He** walked straight past Julie and out to the street.
5. 'I see,' I said slowly, and walked out of **his** office.
6. … **that** said: 'Casa Dorada, El Mayor'.
7. **It** was above my head.
8. **That** was the last thing I remembered.

2 Match the verbs in list A with the words and phrases in list B. Then write the phrases.

	A	B	
1	look	a jacket	1 *look in the mirror*
2	ring	goodbye	2
3	search	the bell	3
4	turn on	in the mirror	4
5	wave	the room	5
6	wear	the stereo	6

3 Complete with these prepositions.

> at   behind   in   on   to   with

1. He was about 25, _____ long brown hair.
2. A young blonde woman in a red suit smiled _____ me.
3. I drove _____ Mark Jackson's apartment.
4. Apartment 132 was _____ the first floor.
5. I heard a man's voice _____ me.
6. I could see the gun _____ the man's hand.

3 You'd better get someone else

1 Look at these sentences from the story. Who or what do the words in bold refer to?

1. 'I got **here** over half an hour ago.'
2. '**It** isn't funny.'
3. Why didn't **she** have a Texas accent?
4. 'He was **there** to pick up a Metro car.'
5. But I knew **one thing** …
6. **We** were alone.
7. 'Why did Vargas lie about **that**?'
8. '… there was a phone call on Monday that scared **him**.'

L.A. BLUES

2 What new information does Ann give Lenny in the story?

_____
_____
_____
_____

3 Complete with these adverbs of manner.

> nervously   properly   quickly   quietly   slowly

1 I couldn't think _____.
2 'I'm sorry, Mr Samuel,' she said _____.
3 When I got there, Julie smiled _____ …
4 … and looked _____ around the office.
5 'Mr Vargas told me not to say anything,' she said _____.

4 I heard someone coming

1 Number these things in the right order.

A Lenny parked outside the Casa Dorada. ☐
B Lenny slept in the back of the car. ☐
C Lenny met Ann at the Roosevelt Hotel. ☐
D Lenny saw a yellow seaplane. ☐
E They had something to eat in a café. ☐
F Hank carried a metal box into the Casa Dorada. ☐
G They drove to Mexico. ☐
H Lenny gave the manager some money. ☐
I Lenny and Ann looked at the guest book. ☐

2 Complete with these prepositions.

> at   for   into   of   near   on   over   with

1 We went _____ a small café.
2 'It's at the end _____ that road.'
3 The Casa Dorada was an old wooden house _____ the water.
4 I rang the bell _____ the desk.
5 A thin, dark-haired man stood _____ the door.
6 'We'd like two cabins _____ the night.'
7 I never argue _____ women.
8 I heard a plane flying _____ the lake.

3 Match the verbs in list A with the words and phrases in list B. Then write the phrases.

	A	B		
1	arrive	asleep	1	_arrive in a town_
2	cross	the border	2	_____
3	fall	the car	3	_____
4	look	some food	4	_____
5	order	through a book	5	_____
6	park	in a town	6	_____

5 Where have you been?

1 Look at these sentences from the story. Who or what do the words in bold refer to?

1 Ann's bag was on the floor, but she wasn't **there**.
   _____
2 'And **I** don't want Hank to see us.'
   _____
3 'Let's do **it** now.'
   _____
4 Then Ann pointed at **something**.
   _____
5 'At least **it's** not Mark.'
   _____
6 'But I'm sure Mark was **here** last week.'
   _____
7 'Perhaps he's **there** now.'
   _____
8 I've taken some photos of **it**.'
   _____

2 Complete with these words and phrases.

> deeply   down   excited   for air   my head   the way

1 asked _____
2 breathed _____
3 came up _____
4 dived _____
5 looked _____
6 shook _____

109

L.A. BLUES

3 Write words from page 102.

three nouns for transport

boat, _____

four verbs to do with seeing

saw, _____

6 It contained thousands of dollars!

1 Answer the questions.

1 Who was in the seaplane on the tenth trip?

2 How did Lenny and Ann get to the *Coromandel*?

3 How did they climb onto the ship?

4 When they first looked down, what could they see on the table?

5 What did the metal box contain?

6 Why did the white-haired man touch the stones with a wet finger?

2 Match the verbs in list A with the words and phrases in list B. Then write the phrases.

	A	B	
1	become	a box	1 *become dark*
2	count	dark	2
3	make	a motorboat	3
4	open	a trip	4
5	rent	the engine	5
6	turn off	the money	6

3 Write sentences describing the picture on page 103.

7 The driver had an accident

1 Number these things in the right order.

A Julie said Dr Summers' clinic rented cars to go to Mexico. ☐

B He drove to Dr Summers' clinic. ☐

C They drove back to L.A. ☐

D She said a driver from the clinic had had an accident. ☐

E Dr Summers and Walter carried a man out of the clinic. ☐

F Ann and Lenny swam to the motorboat. ☐

G Lenny guessed the dead man in the lake was the driver. ☐

H Lenny went to ask Julie some questions. ☐

2 Complete with these verbs.

| drove | finds | go | got | looked | turned | woke |

1 I _____ on the engine.

2 'It's time to _____ back to L.A.'

3 When I _____ up, it was morning.

4 'Walter will kill us both if he _____ out we've talked to anyone!'

5 I _____ up Dr Summers in the phone book.

6 Suddenly, a white Cadillac _____ up and a man _____ out.

3 Write five questions about the story to ask another student in class.

8 I should have guessed!

1 Look at these sentences from the story. Who or what do the words in bold refer to?

1 **It** was Mark Jackson.

2 'Where did **you** hide the diamonds?'

3 '**They**'ve got Mark!'

4 As **we** drove to El Mayor …

5 Then the seaplane flew **them** to the Casa Dorada.

6 'Let **me** kill him!'

7 There's **a woman** in the water!

8 **A man with long brown hair** was lying on the floor.

L.A. BLUES

2 Complete with these words.

> asked   reply   shouted   tell   told

1 Jackson didn't – or couldn't – _____.
2 'Be outside the hotel in half an hour,' I _____ her.
3 'What do you mean?' Ann _____ angrily.
4 'You again!' he _____.
5 'Now _____ me what's going on.'

9 The L.A. blues had gone!

1 Answer the questions.

Who …

1 was smuggling diamonds?
2 found and hid the diamonds?
3 took Mark Jackson to the clinic?
4 held a gun to Ann's head?
5 pulled Ann into the boat?
6 dived to the bottom of the lake?
7 were told to kill Ann and Lenny?
8 killed Hank?
9 phoned the Mexican police?
10 worked for the US Customs?

2 Write words from pages 106 and 107.

1 found out _____
2 area where water reaches land _____
3 opposite of *shook his head* _____
4 walked like soldiers _____
5 hair between the nose and the mouth _____
6 evidence to show that something is true _____
7 someone who illegally takes goods across borders _____
8 killer _____

3 Complete with these prepositions and adverbs.

> at   back   by   for   from   in   into
> of   on   to   under   up   with

1 'The diamonds are _____ the bottom of the lake, _____ the flag.'
2 He took the boat _____ the middle of the lake, stopped _____ the flag, and Ann dived _____.
3 Finally, she came _____ with a box in her hands.
4 The boat came _____ to the shore.
5 'Take Samuel and the girl _____ a walk.'
6 Captain Jimenez turned _____ Ann.
7 'This young lady is _____ the US Customs and she called us _____ her phone.'
8 'The Mexican police work closely _____ the US Customs.
9 'You're full _____ surprises,' I said.

CLIL ART AFTER 2 Pop Art

1 Vocabulary

Match the names of the different art techniques below with the pictures A-F.

1 oil painting

2 silk screen print

3 collage

4 comic strip

5 graphic design

6 sculpture

2 Reading

Read *All about Pop Art* and match the correct heading with each paragraph.

> Aims and criticisms   A definition
> Pop Art in the USA
> Pop Art in the UK   The origins

All about POP ART

1 *A definition*

Pop Art is a movement which is based on images of everyday consumer goods like domestic products, and popular culture like films, pop music or comics. It depicts simple images of common objects with bright, bold colours, which look like modern graphic design. This is thanks to techniques like collage or repetition, as well as modern materials like acrylic paints in fluorescent or metallic colours. In Pop Art, how you communicate is as important as the subject of the picture.

2

American art critic and curator, Lawrence Alloway, was the first to use the term, Pop Art, to refer to a new, more accessible form of popular art. It emerged from the British and American cultures of New York and London between the 1950s and 1960s. However, Pop Art has its origins in the Dada movement of the 1920s. Both movements questioned society and its values. They both developed techniques such as photomontage, collage and assembly of ready-made objects, previously not considered as real art.

3

Pop Art brought art to a wider public, promoting a mass-produced, everyday art which everybody could understand. Many of its concepts are copied from the media or from advertising. Pop Art celebrates and criticises a modern society based on money and what you can buy. Critics describe it as vulgar, sensationalist and not true art; but love it or hate it, Pop Art reflects an era's obsession with beautiful things and people.

4

In the USA, Roy Lichtenstein produced stylised comic strips on giant canvases, using strong primary colours (red, blue, yellow), thick black lines and dots. The best-known American Pop Artist is probably Andy Warhol. He created silk-screen prints from photographs of famous people like Marilyn Monroe and Michael Jackson and objects like tins of soup and Coca-Cola bottles. He copied the same images to make them dull and empty; a view of America's materialist culture. There were also sculptors like the Swedish-born Claes Oldenburg, who created soft giant plastic sculptures of things like hamburgers, ice cream, typewriters and baths.

5

The most iconic British work of Pop Art is probably Richard Hamilton's collage called 'Just what is it that makes today's homes so different, so appealing?' It is full of the characteristics of modern life: cars, comics, newspapers, beautiful people, TV, films, domestic appliances and advertising. Another famous British Pop Artist is David Hockney. His pictures are realist and minimalist, often based on photographs, and they use light in a very distinctive way. Some of them show scenes with people, but others don't.

3 Vocabulary

Match these words with their definitions.

> canvas   critic   curator   depict   dot   minimalist   realist   stylized

1 A person who writes opinions about art, books, films or plays.   *critic*
2 A person who looks after the objects in a museum.
3 In a style that is artificial rather than realistic.
4 To describe someone or something using words or pictures.
5 Material on which artists paint with oil paints.
6 A very small spot of ink or colour.
7 A work of art that shows life as it really is.
8 A style of art that uses simple shapes and colours.

4 Quiz

Part 1

Read *All about Pop Art* again. For each number 1–8, choose word or phrase A, B, C or D.

1 **Pop Art** is a movement based on images from
- A comics.
- B domestic products.
- C films.
- D all of these.

2 **Pop Art** uses
- A dark colours.
- B neutral colours.
- C fluorescent colours.
- D light colours.

3 In **Pop Art**, how you communicate is
- A as important as the subject.
- B less important than the subject.
- C more important that the subject.
- D the only important thing.

4 Lawrence Alloway was
- A a Pop Artist.
- B British.
- C the first critic to talk about Pop Art.
- D the curator of the first Pop Art museum.

5 **Pop Art** and Dada
- A agreed with the values of society.
- B developed new artistic techniques.
- C were fine art movements.
- D were 1920s art movements.

6 **Pop Art** works are
- A accessible.
- B complicated.
- C exclusive.
- D unique.

7 **Pop Art**'s approach to a society based on money and buying things was
- A generally negative.
- B generally positive.
- C neither positive or negative.
- D positive and negative.

8 **Pop Art** reflects an era which was obsessed with
- A beauty.
- B sensationalism.
- C truth.
- D vulgarity.

Part 2

Match the artists with the techniques they used.

1. Andy Warhol ☐
2. Claes Oldenburg ☐
3. David Hockney ☐
4. Richard Hamilton ☐
5. Roy Lichtenstein ☐

- a Collages full of the characteristics of modern life.
- b Realist and minimalist, based on photographs and using light in a distinctive way.
- c Silk-screen prints from photographs of famous people and everyday goods.
- d Stylized comic strips on giant canvases, using strong primary colours, thick black lines and dots.
- e Soft giant plastic sculptures of fast food and household items.

5 Project work

You are a Pop Art critic. Search for one of the Pop Artists on the Internet and find more information about him or her. Write a critical piece about one of his works. Remember to include:

- information about his life
- a description of the artist's style and techniques
- a detailed analysis of the work of art
- your own opinion about the work of art, with reasons why you like or dislike it

CLIL SCIENCE
4 The human brain

1 Quiz
Read the sentences and guess if they are correct. Write *T* (true) or *F* (false).

1. The adult human brain weighs about 1.4 kg.
2. The brain controls everything we do and who we are.
3. We have 100 billion brain cells called neurons in our brain.
4. The cells in our brain are connected and transmit messages a million times a second.
5. Our brain cells transmit messages at a speed of over 500km an hour.
6. Our brain only develops according to the biological information inherited from our parents.
7. Our brain stops working when we are asleep.
8. We only use 10% of our brain.
9. The right part of the brain controls the right part of the body.
10. Unlike other cells, brain cells cannot be renewed when they are dead or damaged.

2 Reading
Read this text and check your answers in exercise 1.

BRAIN FACTS AND BRAIN FICTION

FACTS

The brain is one of the largest organs of the human body, weighing about 1.4 kg in an adult. It is the most complex organ, controlling everything we do and everything we are. It does this with the help of 100 billion (100,000,000,000) nerve cells called neurons. These connect with each other a million times a second to send messages to the brain through electrical and chemical signals transmitted at over 240km per hour. This activity shapes each of our brains in a unique way. Although we may start life with a certain set of genes inherited from our parents, it is our life experiences that determine how our brain develops and changes and consequently what type of person we will become.

FICTION

Our brain never stops working, even when we are asleep. It uses up 20% of the body's total energy. It is a myth that we only use 10% of our brain. In fact, we use 100% of our brain so that our mind and body function correctly. Damage to even small parts of the brain due to accident or illness can cause serious disability. Another strange thing is that the left hemisphere seems to control the right part of the body and the right hemisphere the left part of the body. This can be seen in people who have strokes affecting one part of the brain and immobilising the opposite part of the body. Scientists believed for a long time that brain cells couldn't be regenerated. However, recent research found that the brain produces neurons throughout our lives, especially in the part of the brain responsible for learning and memory.

3 Vocabulary
Complete the sentences with the appropriate form of these words from the text.

| gene   hemisphere   neuron   ~~organ~~   regenerate   stroke |

1. The largest _organ_ in the human body isn't the brain but the skin.
2. We have around a hundred billion _____ in our brain.
3. The _____ we get from our parents determine things like the colour of our eyes.
4. The two _____ of the brain are responsible for making the opposite sides of the body work.
5. People have a _____ when a part of the brain doesn't get enough oxygen from the blood, and it can cause loss of speech or movement.
6. Scientists believe you can help _____ brain cells by taking exercise and eating a healthy diet.

4 Reading and writing

Read *Brain Power* about the different functions of the brain and complete the diagram with these words and phrases.

> brain stem   cerebellum   cerebrum   diencephalon   frontal lobe   limbic system   meninges   parietal lobe

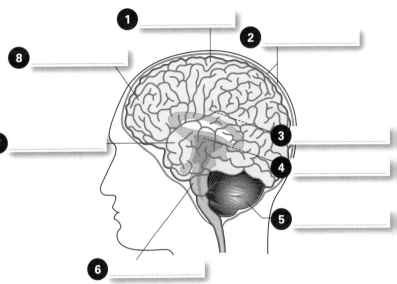

Have you ever wondered how you ride your bike or remember your favourite song? Well that's all thanks to your incredible brain, which is made up of several different parts, each with its own job to do.

The cerebrum is the main part of the brain, which thinks and controls voluntary muscles. It is divided into left and right hemispheres, which are in communication with each other, and several separate sections called lobes. The frontal lobe of the cerebrum helps us speak, think, feel and coordinate our movements, like kicking a football. In the middle, there's the parietal lobe controlling our sense of touch and telling us when to feel pain and temperature. At the back of the cerebrum is the occipital lobe, which is involved in sight. Left and right of the cerebrum are the temporal lobes, responsible for sound and memory – your favourite songs!

The second biggest part of the brain, the cerebellum, is at the back of the skull under the cerebrum. This is the part of the brain responsible for accuracy, equilibrium and coordination. Staying on your skateboard without falling off or putting your contact lenses in are possible thanks to the cerebellum. The brain stem is just under the cerebellum, connecting the brain to the spinal cord. This is responsible for all the body's vital, involuntary processes like breathing, digestion and circulation of the blood and is also responsible for monitoring sleep. The limbic system, at the centre of the brain, manages emotions and instincts and so is vital to reading situations and to recognising when you're in danger.

The diencephalon lies on top of the brain stem and just under the centre of the cerebrum.

One part of the brain, the hypothalamus, oversees the general conditions of the body, like if you're hot, cold, hungry or thirsty. It also controls your metabolism. The other part, the thalamus, acts like a switchboard, organising all the incoming messages and directing them to the correct part of the brain. Around the brain, protecting it from disease and providing it with energy, there is a clear liquid called the cerebrospinal fluid. Outside this, are three membranes, or hard tissue called meninges, and finally there is the skull made of bone, all of which protect the brain from injury.

5 Vocabulary

Write definitions of the words and phrases in the box in exercise 4, saying what each part of the brain does.

6 Project work

Search for 'human brain' on the Internet and find out more about it. Design a colourful poster for your class and name it *Look after your brain*. Include information about:

- what is good for your brain and why
- what is bad for your brain and why

CLIL HISTORY
AFTER 6 Inventions that shaped our world

1 Quiz

For each question 1–10, choose word or phrase A, B or C.

1. Jeans were originally designed as
   A   a fashion accessory.
   B   clothes for work.
   C   clothes for special occasions.

2. Levi Strauss was
   A   a gold miner.
   B   a fashion designer.
   C   an immigrant worker.

3. The Chinese invented a toothbrush made of
   A   bamboo and pig's hairs.
   B   bone and dog's hair.
   C   wood and grass.

4. The first electric toothbrush was available on the market in the
   A   1940s.
   B   1960s.
   C   1980s.

5. Plastic has taken over because it's
   A   durable and less heavy.
   B   less expensive.
   C   safe and clean.

6. The time it takes plastic to biodegrade is
   A   14 years.
   B   145 years.
   C   450 years.

7. The first ever text message sent said:
   A   Happy birthday!
   B   Hi there!
   C   Merry Christmas!

8. The percentage of people in the world today with a mobile phone is
   A   50%.
   B   60%.
   C   70%.

9. The Internet was originally developed by the US government as a
   A   business network.
   B   research network.
   C   social network.

10. The percentage of the world's population today with access to the Internet is
    A   30%.
    B   40%.
    C   50%.

2 Reading

Read the text and check your answers in exercise 2.

Have you ever considered where jeans come from and who invented them? They were originally designed by Levi Strauss, a young German-Jewish immigrant living in the USA during the American Gold Rush. They were intended as practical clothes for men working in the mines, so they were made of a strong cotton from France called 'Serge de Nimes'. That's why the material is called denim today. Levi's® blue jeans were officially patented in 1873 and have since become very popular all around the world.

Believe it or not, in ancient times people used to brush their teeth with wooden sticks! It was not until 1498 that the Chinese came up with a kind of toothbrush with a bamboo handle and pig's hairs. In 1938, the modern toothbrush was invented by Dupont de Nemours, an industrial research laboratory in the USA, thanks to the accidental discovery of nylon in 1930 by Dr Wallace Carothers, an American scientist working for them at the time. A year later the first electric toothbrush was developed by the Swiss and was later made available on the American market in the 1960s.

Soft drinks like lemonade used to be sold either in glass bottles or in tin cans. Plastic has replaced them because it is more durable, light and transparent. The first type of plastic, celluloid, was used for making analogue camera films. It was discovered and manufactured in 1872 by John Hyatt in the USA. Because it was highly flammable it was replaced by bakelite in radios and telephones in the 1930s. Today many different products are made of chemically produced plastics, like PET for bottles of water and PVC for credit cards and footballs. Unfortunately, it takes 450 years for one plastic bottle to biodegrade!

Imagine life without text messaging! Although American Motorola introduced the world's first portable handheld phone in 1983, the Short Messaging Service (SMS) wasn't developed until the late 1980s in the UK by Vodafone™. The first message was sent on 3rd December 1992 by Neil Papworth and that message was 'Merry Christmas!' Nowadays the number of text messages sent annually is almost one trillion (1,000,000,000,000) amongst the approximately 4 million users (60% of the world's population). Texting has become more popular than calling on the phone. You can even send photos in a text message.

The Internet has revolutionised the way we learn, communicate, relax and interact with the world around us. But where did it all begin? The US government developed a network called ARPANET in 1969, linking different university research departments. However it was in 1989 that Tim Berners-Lee, an Englishman working in Switzerland, developed the World Wide Web which provides access to data on computers all over the world through the network of networks called the Internet. It is estimated that 50% of the world's population now have Internet access.

3 Reading and writing

Complete the chart with information from the text in exercise 3.

Invention	Inventor	Place and date of invention	Past developments	Recent developments
		USA, 1873	Clothes for men working in the mines during the Gold Rush	
	Dupont de Nemours			Electric toothbrush
		USA, 1872		Many different goods like films, credit cards and bottles
Text messaging			Motorola's hand held mobile phone	
	Tim Berners-Lee		ARPANET	

4 Vocabulary

Match the words and phrases. Write sentences comparing the present and the past.

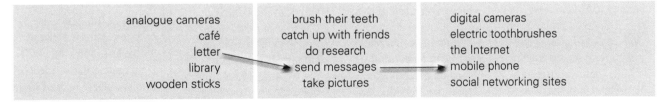

People used to send letters, but now they send text messages with their mobile phones.

5 Project work

Search for an invention that has shaped your life. Write a description of it but don't mention its name. The other students will try to guess what it is. Remember to include information about:

- who invented it
- when and where it was invented
- past developments that led to the invention
- recent developments
- why you think it is so important to your life

AFTER 8 — CLIL NATURAL SCIENCE

Forces of nature

1 Reading

Read *Natural Disasters*. Then match the texts with the pictures.

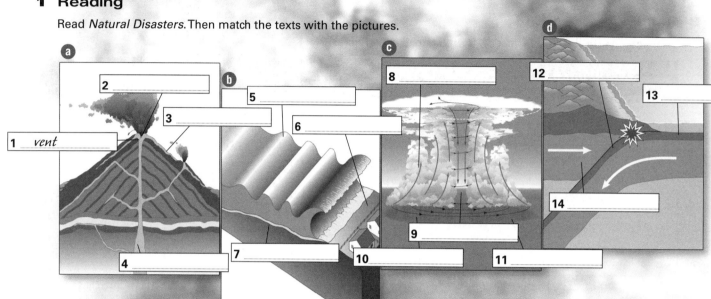

NATURAL DISASTERS

1 ☐
Tropical storms are called 'hurricanes' in the Atlantic Ocean, 'cyclones' in the Indian Ocean, and 'typhoons' in the Pacific Ocean. They are powerful storms, moving in a clockwise direction north of the equator, from July to September, and in an anticlockwise direction south of the equator, from January to March every year. They are formed when low atmospheric pressure meets warm air evaporating from the sea and result in high winds and heavy rains moving across the surface of the ocean at 120 to 320 kph. The results can be flooding, destruction of land and buildings and loss of life. Cyclone Nargis struck Myanmar (Burma) in South East Asia on 2 May 2008, killing an estimated 138,000 people and destroying the livelihoods of many more.

2 ☐
Earthquakes occur when big pieces of rock, called tectonic plates, making up the outer layer of the Earth, the crust, pull against each other. They're pulled towards Earth's inner layer, the core, forming cracks. Friction from the rubbing of the plates along these cracks creates energy which is released in the form of an earthquake when the tectonic plates get free of each other. When an earthquake strikes, you feel the ground moving, and then you see objects falling and buildings collapsing. On 12 January 2010, Haiti in the Caribbean suffered an earthquake of magnitude 7 out of 10 on the Richter scale. Approximately 316,000 people died and 1.5 million people were made homeless.

3 ☐
The word tsunami is from the Japanese words for harbour wave. It describes the experience of a sudden giant wave hitting the land. Tsunamis are the result of the underwater movement caused by earthquakes or volcanic eruptions. This leads to the fast movement of long but not very high waves in the deep, open ocean, not always easy to detect. Once the tsunami reaches land, the waves get faster and higher, up to 30 metres high. These giant waves destroy everything in their path, like the Sumatran tsunami in the Indian Ocean on 26 December, 2004. It was caused by an earthquake of 8.9 Richter. About 225,000 people died in the coastal areas because they had no warning and no time to escape.

4 ☐
A volcanic eruption pushes hot gas, rock, ash and lava (melted rock) out through the opening or vent of a mountain below or above the surface of the Earth. Magma, hot liquid rock, is pushed out through cracks between the Earth's crust and core. Different types of explosion can cause changes in the weather, damage to surrounding areas or loss of life. Volcanic eruptions can be Icelandic, where lava flows slowly from quite a flat surface, or Plinian, where a lot of lava, rock and toxic gas are ejected violently upwards through the crack. On 25 November 1985, the eruption of Mount Ruiz in Columbia killed 25,000 people. Volcanologists predict eruptions by monitoring the seismic activity around a volcano, but it is difficult to evacuate populated areas and to predict the earthquakes that precede eruptions.

2 Vocabulary

Read *Natural Disasters* again. Label the pictures in exercise 1 with these words and phrases.

> crater   crust   fault   heavy rain   high winds   lava   low pressure
> magma   seabed   shore   tectonic plates   ~~vent~~   warm air   wave

3 Quiz
NATURAL DISASTERS

For each question 1–10, choose word or phrase A, B, C or D.

1 Tropical storms are also called
- **A** cyclones.
- **B** hurricanes.
- **C** typhoons.
- **D** all of these.

2 Tropical cyclones south of the equator occur from
- **A** January to March, moving anticlockwise.
- **B** January to March, moving clockwise.
- **C** July to September, moving anticlockwise.
- **D** July to September, moving clockwise.

3 Tropical cyclones can travel at a speed of
- **A** 25 to 50 kph.
- **B** 75 to 100 kph.
- **C** 120 to 320 kph.
- **D** 300 to 550 kph.

4 Earthquakes are caused due to the movement of big rocks
- **A** in the Earth's core.
- **B** in the Earth's crust.
- **C** in the Earth's mantle.
- **D** on top of the Earth.

5 Earthquakes are measured using a scale referred to as
- **A** Australian.
- **B** Icelandic.
- **C** Plinian.
- **D** Richter.

6 An earthquake happens when the plates
- **A** get close to each other.
- **B** are separated.
- **C** break.
- **D** are rubbed.

7 *Tsunami* is a Japanese word meaning
- **A** 'harbour wave'.
- **B** 'killer wave'.
- **C** 'land wave'.
- **D** 'ocean wave'.

8 When a tsunami reaches the shore, the waves are
- **A** faster and higher.
- **B** faster and shorter.
- **C** slower and higher.
- **D** slower and shorter.

9 Which of the following is not forced out during a volcanic eruption?
- **A** lava
- **B** rock
- **C** toxic gas
- **D** water

10 Volcanologists can predict
- **A** the creation of volcanoes.
- **B** eruptions of existing volcanoes.
- **C** earthquakes.
- **D** where the lava will go.

4 Project work

Search for a major natural disaster on the Internet. Prepare a presentation with pictures, diagrams and lots of facts. Remember to include information about:

- when and where it happened
- how it happened
- what the effects were (on the people, the environment, the climate, the economy, etc.)
- what could be done to prevent the disastrous consequences if it happens again

Macmillan Education Limited
4 Crinan Street
London N1 9XW

Companies and representatives throughout the world

ISBN 978-0-230-41256-9

Text © Judy Garton-Sprenger and Philip Prowse 2012
Additional text by Helena Gomm and Catrin Morris 2012
Design and illustration © Macmillan Education Limited 2012

This edition published 2012
First edition published 2006

All rights reserved; no part of this publication may be reproduced, stored in a retrieval system, transmitted in any form, or by any means, electronic, mechanical, photocopying, recording, or otherwise, without the prior written permission of the publishers.

Original design by Giles Davies Design Limited
Page make-up by D&J Hunter Design
Illustrated by Ilias Arahovitis (Beehive) p26; John Dillow p36*b*; Mark Duffin p56; Peter Harper p115; Bob Harvey (Pennant Illustration Agency, pp98-106; Zakir Hussein (Advocate Art) p36*t*; Tim Kahane p68; Peter Lubach pp28-29; Gillian Martin pp6, 38, 71, 83, 88; Julian Mosedale pp15, 33, 47, 62-63, 67, 78-79; Julia Pearson p7; David Semple pp30*r*, 41; Simon Smith pp30*l*, 87; Redgiraffe pp74-75, 86*r*; John Richardson p44; Mark Ruffle p42; Harry Venning pp50, 64, 86*l*; Simon Williams (Illustrationweb) p36*m*; and Gary Wing p18.
Cover design by Designers Collective
Cover photos by Art Directors & Trip/NASA; Corbis/Scott Markewitz/Aurora Photos, Corbis/Carlos Villoch/Specialist Stock; Getty/ASP; Photolibrary/Yvette Cardozo; Rex/KPA/Zuma; Superstock/Photoalto.

The author and publishers would like to thank the following for permission to reproduce their photographs:
Alamy pp56(b), 84(ml), Alamy/Allstar Picture Library p24, Alamy/ARGO Images p60(t), Alamy/Ian M Butterfield (Concepts) p66(tl), Alamy/Allik Camazine p66(cl), Alamy/Design Pics Inc p56(b), Alamy/Dinodia Photos p77, Alamy/Tim Graham p32(t), Alamy/Nigel Hicks p54(t), Alamy/Richard Levine p113(r), Alamy/Mary Evans Picture Library p84(cl), Alamy/Jeff Morgan 16 p61, Alamy/qaphotos.com p32(b), Alamy/Ian Sanders p84(tl), Alamy/Vicki Wagner p76, Alamy/Martin Wierink p117(c); **Ardea**/John Daniels p74; **CORBIS** p114, Corbis/Heide Benser p4(l), Corbis/Christie's Images/DACS p20(c), Corbis/Randy Faris p28, Corbis/Peter Turnley p8(b); **Getty**/AFP p84(r), Denny Allen p60(b), Getty/Ulf Andersen p36(2), Getty/Archive Photos p23, Getty/ASP p6, Getty/ComStock p72, Getty/Dorling Kindersley p117(r), Getty/George Doyle p64(b), Getty/Lonnie Duka p64(t), Getty/Grant Faint p66(tr), Getty/fuer Harald and Erhard Fotografie p4(r), Getty/Aaron Foster p48(t), Getty/Ian Gavan/GP p12(b), Getty/Tom Grill p16(r), Getty Image News p8(r), Getty/Todd Gipstein p92, Getty/IMAGEMORE Co, Ltd. p112(l), Getty/Ron Levine p40, Getty/National Geographic p113(mr), Getty/NY Daily News via Getty Images p66(cr), Getty/PhotoAlto/Sigrid Olsson pp16(l), 19, 22, Getty/Popperfoto p52, Getty/Marco Secchi p36(1), Getty/Stockbyte p117(l); LS Lowry *Man Lying on a Wall* 1957 © The Lowry Collection, Salford p20(b); **J.Ishida** p112(r); **Macmillan Reader covers**: Alamy/Christo Gary Lieghty/Stock Connection – Blue p33, Corbis pp21, 57, Corbis/Tom Brakefield – The Stock Conne/Science Fiction p91, Corbis/Engraving of Kitley House by R. Ackerman, 1828 p81, Getty/Stone p9, Illustration by Matilda Harrison p45, Mark Oldroyd p44, Photodisc Red p93, Punchstock/Photographers Choice p69; **MACMILLAN SOUTH AFRICA** p115; **Mary Evans Picture Library** p36(3); **Photolibrary**/SGM SGM p56(t); **Rex Features**/Alain Lockyer p62, Rex Features/c. Paramount/Everett p80, Rex Features p54(b), Rex/Roger-Viollet p84(r), Rex Features/Sipa Press pp12(t), 50; Rex Features/Cameron Richardson/Newspix p59; **Robert Harding World Imagery**/age footstock p90; **The Bridgeman Art Library**/Au Rendez-Vous des Amis, 1922 (oil on canvas), Ernst, Max (1891-1976)/Ludwig Museum, Cologne, Germany/© DACS /The Bridgeman Art Library p20(t), Bridgeman/Costanza Bonarelli, detail of a sculpture by Gian Lorenzo Bernini (1598-1680) (marble),/Bargello, Florence, Italy /Bridgeman Giraudon p113(ml), Bridgeman/Van Gogh's Bedroom at Arles, 1889 (oil on canvas), Gogh, Vincent van (1853-90)/The Art Institute of Chicago, IL, USA /Bridgeman Giraudon p113(l); **The Picture Desk**/DREAMWORKS ANIMATION/THE KOBAL COLLECTION p14(m), The Picture Desk/SEE-SAW FILMS/THE KOBAL COLLECTION p14(l), The Picture Desk/UK FILM COUNCIL/AEGIS FILM FUND/PRESIENCE/THE KOBAL COLLECTION p14(r). **Science Photo Library**/Lynette Cook p48(b)

Commissioned photography by Lisa Payne p2.

The authors and publishers are grateful for permission to include the following copyright material.
Page 44: Material extracted from *The Woman Who Disappeared* by Philip Prowse a *Macmillan Guided Reader*, copyright © Philip Prowse 1975, 1992, 1998, 2002 & 2005, reprinted by permission of Macmillan Education;
Page 61: Poem 'The Tourists Are Coming' taken from *Wicked World* (Penguin Books, 2000), copyright © Benjamin Zephaniah 2000, reprinted by permission the publisher on behalf of Benjamin Zephaniah;
Page 72: 'African Dream' by Martin Prowse copyright © Martin Prowse 2006, reprinted by permission of the author;
Page 24: Extract from 'Teenage kicks' by Sam Wetherell copyright © Sam Wetherell 2004 first published in *The Guardian* 25.06.04.

These materials may contain links for third-party websites. We have no control over, and are not responsible for, the contents of such third-party websites. Please use care when accessing them.

Although we have tried to trace and contact copyright holders before publication, in some cases this has not been possible. If contacted, we will be pleased to rectify any errors or omissions at the earliest opportunity.

Printed and bound in Poland by CGS

2025   2024   2023   2022
41   40   39   38   37   36   35